# Nonprofit Leadership Development

What's Your "Plan A"
for Growing Future Leaders?

By Kirk Kramer and Preeta Nayak

The Bridgespan Group would like to thank Omidyar Network,
the David and Lucile Packard Foundation, and Deerbrook Charitable
Trust for their support in making this research possible.

**ON**
OMIDYAR NETWORK™

the David &
Lucile Packard
FOUNDATION

DEERBROOK
CHARITABLE TRUST

# Table of Contents

# Foreword

**By Sal Giambanco, Partner, Human Capital, Omidyar Network**

When the elevator door opens at Omidyar Network's headquarters in Redwood City, you are greeted by the following quotation, neatly lettered on the wall:

*"Every individual has the power to make a difference."*

Nine words that are paradoxically simple and complicated. Indeed, every person does have the power to make a difference if they can avail themselves of the ways and means to do so. Therein lies the essence of what we do every day at Omidyar Network: focus on the conditions that enable opportunity and choice for individuals, bridging the gap between what is and what could be.

Our fundamental starting point is that all people are inherently good and capable; if given the opportunity to tap their unique talents, an individual can materially improve his or her own well-being, thereby catalyzing meaningful change for her family and community. To us, it is eminently obvious that, if you start with the most basic unit—the human being—the rest will follow.

That might sound a bit lofty or idealistic but, to us, it is just a smart operating principle that is grounded in our real-world experience and sound social science. We were founded by Pierre Omidyar and his wife, Pam. Pierre also created eBay, which, since its humble beginnings in 1995, has broken down the barriers-to-entry for millions of individual entrepreneurs around the world, enabling them to make a living by providing products and services that create value.

When Pierre was getting eBay off the ground, more important than early seed capital was the human capital support he received from investors. Early investors provided value beyond funding at a critical time when eBay was scaling rapidly. These investors had significant business experience and networks, enabling them to provide coaching, make connections to key industry experts, and identify people to fill skill gaps. Learning from this experience, Omidyar Network was structured to provide similar support to its investees and grantees. At Omidyar Network, we know that financial capital is critically important, but we are equally convinced that support of human capital, grounded by leadership development, is just as critical—if not more so.

Consistently, our grantees and investees communicate an urgent need for leadership development and talent management, and we have oriented our human capital efforts accordingly. Organizations invite Omidyar Network to help identify future leaders, hone the skills of existing management teams, and develop plans that will help their organizations scale up. Specific projects relative to leadership have included executive and board recruiting, executive coaching, succession planning, and talent management training. Our experience, and that of our grantees and investees, clearly indicates that the stronger the leadership team, the higher the organizational performance and the greater the progress toward social impact goals and mission achievement.

The Bridgespan Group has been a key partner in these leadership development efforts since our founding. Together, we have set out to tackle some of the thorniest issues any organization faces: how to attract, retain, and nurture first-rate leaders. Social change organizations, in particular, can really struggle with these challenges. While resource constraints are a contributing factor, we have found it is not "just" about money. *Nonprofit Leadership Development: What's Your "Plan A" for Growing Future Leaders?* sets out a straightforward road map to enable an organization to set up systems and structures that will enable it to approach leadership development strategically and proactively, thereby transforming the "burdens" of talent management into—dare I say it—a joyful and fulfilling process.

When the leadership and talent pieces fall into place, performance in all functions is improved, from marketing to fundraising to service delivery to client retention. Yet, more often than not, organizational leaders make the fatal mistake of relegating leadership development and talent management to the sidelines, viewing it as an administrative afterthought or a luxury that the organization can't afford to do in a high-quality way. It's akin to spending more time worrying about whether the copiers have enough toner than if the human beings are sufficiently inspired.

These otherwise capable and passionate leaders take this approach in spite of the fact that time and again, empirical evidence is proving that the most innovative, effective, and sustainable organizations are those that make leadership development a real and measurable priority. They deliver on that priority by ensuring their holistic employee value proposition is both a magnet for the right people and a lab for a meaningful and exciting career. We know this because we see it borne out every day in our partner and investee organizations. The best-run organizations are those where the head of an organization embraces her role as chief talent officer.

At Omidyar Network, we have dedicated a lot of time, energy, and financial resources to human capital and leadership development. And we plan to commit substantially more. We see this as the smartest investment that can be made in humanity. Leadership development can have a true multiplier effect; thereby enabling the scale we believe is required to achieve real and lasting change.

Of course, none of this is easy. If it were, we would have all figured it out long ago. The factors at play are myriad, complex, and entrenched. And yet, as we begin to learn more and identify replicable best practices, we are starting to see the beginnings of a leadership breakthrough at many of the organizations with which we partner. *Nonprofit Leadership Development: What's Your "Plan A" for Growing Future Leaders?* will now become an integral part of our leadership toolbox. We urge organizations of all shapes and sizes to take its recommendations to heart—and in so doing, enable each individual in the organization to make the most powerful difference she can.

# Introduction: What's Your Plan A?

*"I am a leader who is actively engaged in finding young talent and developing new leaders, but I find myself alone in this at our company..."*
*– COO, community improvement organization*

*"[Leadership development] has never been [our] focus before. It is now, but the single biggest barrier is getting the infrastructure in place to support what we say we now want to do."*
*– CEO, international NGO*

*"Our agency knows leadership development is important, but figuring out how to do it and making the time when we are at capacity is the difficult part."*
*– Executive team member, mental health organization*

*"We may have a decent idea of where we want the organization to go, but we have no idea what people will be required to get us there."*
*– Board member, youth development organization*

*"Potential leaders are often so busy working on the front lines that they don't have the time to put into really developing leadership skills."*
*– Manager, human services organization*

*"Financial resources [are] limited, and meeting our internal business goals (i.e., survival) is a higher priority than leadership development."*
*– CEO, international NGO*

Do any of these statements sound familiar? Here at The Bridgespan Group, our work brings us into contact with a wide variety of nonprofits, from national networks with well-known brands and nine-figure budgets to start-ups running on little more than the zeal of a few founders. Wherever we go we hear the same themes running through the conversations: Leadership development is hard. There's never enough time. And how can anyone invest in leadership development when they need every incremental dollar to keep programs running?

It's true that investment in leadership can feel like a luxury compared with investing in services at the heart of a nonprofit's mission, such as opening another after-school mentoring site, protecting another thousand acres of rainforest, or securing more housing for low-income families. But failure to invest in leadership as well as services puts the entire mission at risk.

And based on our research, it's a risk that's unnecessary. In our work with nonprofits and especially in conversations with nonprofit leaders, we found chief executive officers (CEOs) and executive directors (EDs) who are effectively working with their senior leadership teams to develop their next generation of leaders (for simplicity's sake, we'll refer throughout this guide to the generic senior leader as the CEO), boards that are actively engaged in long-term leadership planning, and organizations that are building the capacity of their line managers to develop future leaders. This guide is designed to share their stories and lessons so that you can do the same for your organization. After you read this guide, we hope you'll find that "what to do" isn't a mystery. Nor should it seem like another "add-on" to your existing work. Rather, our hope is that you will be well equipped to integrate the work of building new leaders into the day-to-day life of your organization.

One of the most important actions you can take to make leadership development a daily activity at your organization is to go through the process of creating a **Plan A** for your organization's senior leaders. We first heard the term, and the philosophy behind it, from Ken Chenault, CEO of American Express. In an intimate discussion with an audience of executives from a dozen nonprofit networks in November 2011, he laid out the tenets of the Plan A approach. We can report without exaggeration that nearly everyone in attendance was nodding vigorously as Chenault walked them through the details.

In essence, Plan A is a vision of your organization's future leadership team (say, three to five years out), including the capabilities and roles needed to achieve your strategy, and an overview of the development steps you plan to take to build that team. You create your Plan A by defining the likely challenges and needs of tomorrow, inferring the leadership qualities required to meet them, and building those qualities systematically in the staff who have true leadership potential. It differs from most succession plans by linking strategy and leadership needs, and by focusing on the future rather than on simply replacing existing positions. For organizations that are growing or evolving in some way, this is a crucial distinction. Once the Plan A for senior leadership is in place, you can begin to extend the process through the rest of the organization.

In this guide, we outline a series of steps that you can follow to create and implement a Plan A as part of your organization's everyday business, inexpensively, and without disrupting the vital work that your organization is doing. While what to do is knowable, we don't promise that it will be easy to do it well. It takes significant focus, time, and effort. But we do say that the actions you take will help build an organization that's better prepared to increase your impact amid the challenges to come.

## Leadership Development: What We Mean and Why It Is Important

When we say "leadership development" we mean the identification and development of those individuals who will lead the critical functions of your organization and who, in partnership with other leaders, will be responsible for its overall health and impact. Bridgespan has long advocated that nonprofits take a much more aggressive stance toward leadership development to prepare for a looming leadership deficit. In a seminal 2006 white paper, "The Nonprofit Sector's Leadership Deficit," Bridgespan co-founder Thomas J. Tierney pointed out that over the coming decade, the nonprofit sector would need to hire as many as 640,000 new senior managers, and by 2016, would need 80,000 new senior managers every year. A follow-up report published in 2009, "Finding Leaders for America's Nonprofits," by David Simms, Carol Trager, and Katie Smith Milway, studied the problem and potential solutions in greater depth. Because their messages resonated so strongly in the nonprofit community, both publications found a wide readership—in fact, "The Nonprofit Sector's Leadership Deficit" remains Bridgespan's most frequently cited publication. This guide builds on the insights contained in those publications, with a particular focus on meeting the leadership challenge by building robust internal pipelines.

We have stressed the importance of leadership over the years because we are committed to increasing the impact of the nonprofit sector. As Tierney wrote in 2006, "[N]onprofits increasingly do the work required to fulfill our desire for a civil, compassionate, well-functioning society. Like most organizations, their ability to consistently deliver these results depends more on the quality of their people than on any other single variable." It's up to leaders to engage their people and organize their energies toward a common goal. Your organization's leaders include the CEO and her direct reports, as well as the managers who run your country operations, your sites, your key programs, your functional departments. And, most important for the purposes of this guide, they include individuals who have the potential to fill these positions. These are the leaders who will carry your organization's mission into the future.

It is in this respect that Plan A and our exploration of leadership development differs from many discussions of succession planning. Most succession plans are concerned primarily with maintaining organizational continuity. They help organizations prepare to fill a current role with a leader whose competencies resemble those of the incumbent. That is a subset of what we discuss. But a Plan A envisions a changed organization that requires new roles, new competencies, or both. It represents an organization's best attempt to answer such questions as: What kind of leaders will the organization need to succeed in the future? Who in the organization has the raw (or somewhat refined) potential to fill those positions? And what does that imply about designing processes, however simple, to develop those leaders internally—starting today? The answers surface the real essentials for the future success of the organization. They go beyond simply replacing current staff or sending future leaders to the occasional training seminar. Rather, they zero in on work experiences that build needed leadership muscle, backed up by mentoring and coaching. Indeed, our research and outside studies show that the most effective kind of leadership development happens primarily on the job, every working day, driven by line managers whose words and actions can stretch the leadership potential of their people—or stifle it.

This guide does not focus on the broader topic of managing the talents of your entire staff. There's nothing here on improving the skills of the front-line social service worker or the functional skills of the accounting manager. Nor do we cover topics such as building community leadership. Those topics, important as they are, are subjects for another day, another guide. Here we focus at the organization-wide level on helping you think about the leaders you need to manage the units that are critical for your future success.

Our work with hundreds of nonprofits over 12 years leads us to conclude that organizations with great leaders maximize the impact of each dollar of investment. Corporate Leadership Council Human Resources, a service of the CEB, finds that leaders who are successful in developing their staff achieve 7 percent more revenue and 6 percent more profit than the average leader, while leaders who are poor developers are 7 and 6 percent below the average.[1] In other words, that's a 14-percentage-point swing between the best and worst developers in revenue and a 12-percentage-point swing in profit. In the nonprofit sector, the Boys and Girls Club of America found that not only did leaders who attended its development training outperform their peers against organizational benchmarks such as youth engagement and retention, but also that investment in leadership development generated a 4-to-1 return.[2]

# The Leadership Development Challenge

Nonprofits are acutely aware of their leadership gaps. Bridgespan has surveyed approximately 500 nonprofit organizations on various aspects of their organizational effectiveness, and the teams we surveyed consistently singled out leadership development and succession planning as their most glaring organizational weakness by a margin of more than two to one. Among respondents to our Leadership Development Diagnostic Survey, only 5 percent strongly agreed and 31 percent agreed that their organizations are "highly effective in developing a strong internal pipeline of future leaders." This finding is echoed in a study by CompassPoint Nonprofit Services, the Annie E. Casey Foundation, the Meyer Foundation, and Idealist.org, which found that nonprofits often hobble their own leadership development efforts, frustrating potential leaders with a "lack of mentorship and support from incumbent executives" and "obscure avenues to career advancement," among other impediments.[3]

---

1 Corporate Leadership Council Human Resources, *Corporate Leadership Council Talent Management Effectiveness Survey.*

2 "Putting a Value on Training," *McKinsey Quarterly*, July 2010.

3 "Ready to Lead? Next Generation Leaders Speak Out," meyerfoundation.org/downloads/ready_to_lead/ReadytoLead2008.pdf.

Nonprofits aren't alone, of course. For-profit companies have their own continuing struggles with leadership development. But nonprofits wrestle with unique resource challenges. Operating under tight restrictions on their overhead and their use of donor funds, many nonprofits have little leeway to invest in their people and infrastructure. Moreover, the struggling national economy and the resulting cuts in public and private funding have put their budgets under even heavier pressure.

Yet we've found that financial resources, or the lack of them, may not be as big an obstacle as the behavior of leaders. However painful it is to admit, many nonprofit leaders (including nonprofit boards) confront the question of leadership development only when the topic is unavoidable—when they have to find a successor to a retiring CEO, for example, or when limited leadership capacity is beginning to hamper the organization's ability to grow and thrive. At times like these, nonprofits suffer because they haven't treated leadership development as an ongoing business process. They haven't recognized that the most successful succession planning is not an episodic event triggered by an executive's departure. Instead, it is a proactive and systematic investment in building a pipeline of leaders within an organization, so that when transitions are necessary, leaders at all levels are ready to answer the call.

In organizations that make such an investment, leadership development becomes part of the culture, a strong thread running through the organization's roster of activities. Building the leaders of tomorrow becomes an integral part of its identity. The key player in forming and fostering that culture is the CEO, whose words and actions, passions and priorities, are a powerful signal to the rest of the organization. Simply put, the organization comes to value what the CEO values. CEOs who visibly invest time, energy, and attention to leadership development—for example by publicly recognizing the leadership development of others, cultivating relationships with high-potential leadership candidates, and above all by spearheading the creation and implementation of the organization's Plan A—send a powerful message that leadership development isn't just the buzz phrase du jour: It's fundamental to the organization's work.

We have created this guide to help nonprofit leaders think differently about leadership development. By changing the way they think, we aspire to change the way they and their organizations approach the discipline of building strong leaders. Our aim is to convince you that leadership development isn't mysterious, accidental, or something that can be postponed. It is, rather, a systematic process that nearly every nonprofit can implement. The time to begin is now, and the tools you need are captured here.

## Diagnosing Your Leadership Development Strengths and Weaknesses

**Before you begin reading this guide, we strongly recommend that you and your senior leadership team complete Bridgespan's Leadership Development Diagnostic Survey, accessible free of charge at www.bridgespan.org/LeadershipDiagnostic.** Based on our research of leadership development best practices in the for-profit and nonprofit sectors, the diagnostic includes 31 questions related to the five core processes described in this guide: engaging your senior leaders, understanding your future needs, developing your future leaders, hiring externally, and monitoring and improving. Taking the survey will help you to assess whether you are being proactive, systematic, and comprehensive in addressing your leadership development and succession planning needs. You are able to compare your responses to others in the sector, and your results will help you decide where to focus your leadership development efforts and what to zero in on when reviewing and learning from the best practices in this guide.

## Steps to Building Future Leaders

Through our research, we discovered certain common elements among organizations that manage leadership development effectively. First and foremost, they are willing to invest in the effort. But what matters more than money is the time and effectiveness of the CEO and senior team in actively managing and promoting development. If senior leaders aren't engaged in coaching, mentoring, and identifying stretch assignments for up-and-coming leaders, no amount of financial investment in outside training can compensate. Beyond investment, we found that the Plan A pros manage leadership development as a core set of activities that become part of the everyday work of their organizations. We identified five linked processes that these organizations perform to animate their Plan As, and we've stitched together the best practices from for-profit and nonprofit organizations for each. We also found that nonprofits of nearly any size can adapt these processes. You don't have to be a large nonprofit with lots of support and resources to execute these basics.

Each chapter in this guide explores one of these processes and suggests action steps for implementing them. Wherever possible, we offer detailed examples of the practices employed at real-life organizations. We also provide samples of tools you can use to implement the processes at your organization. Here's what you'll find in each of the guide's six chapters:

- **Chapter 1—Engaging Your Senior Leaders.** In organizations that build leaders for the long term, the CEO is the de facto chief talent officer—in other words, she drives the leadership development process. She benefits greatly by developing other leaders who over time are able to take on tasks the CEO once performed, freeing her up to focus on other challenges. This chapter explains how her active engagement signals the importance of leadership development to the entire organization. She gets the ball rolling by working to develop her senior leadership team and holding them accountable for developing their direct reports. It's also her job to determine when and how to engage the board in leadership development—if she doesn't, the board is likely to remain a bystander, to the detriment of the overall effort. By taking these steps—and above all by demonstrating energetic, sustained engagement in leadership development—she's planting the seeds of an organizational culture that recognizes and harnesses the transformational power of leadership.

- **Chapter 2—Understanding Your Future Needs.** Organizations that successfully develop future leaders regularly identify how the organization of tomorrow may differ from today's. Indeed, without a clear vision of the organization's future, it will be all but impossible to identify appropriate leadership candidates and design and implement the activities that will develop the skills they'll need to succeed under new circumstances. In this chapter, we discuss the collaborative process your senior team can use to identify leadership candidates, focusing less on their performance than on their potential. This is an absolutely essential undertaking for any organization looking to move beyond simply replacing current leaders on an ad hoc basis toward creating a robust and effective leadership pipeline designed to meet future needs.

- **Chapter 3—Developing Your Future Leaders.** Leaders are not born, they're made. And they're made primarily through well-designed on-the-job experiences, supported by mentoring, coaching, and formal training. More specifically, research has shown that 70 percent on-the-job learning, 20 percent coaching and mentoring, and 10 percent formal training may be the optimum mix for leadership development, and in this chapter we describe how organizations like the YMCA of the USA (Y-USA) systematically develop their talent by blending "stretch" opportunities, coaching, and formal learning within the 70-20-10 framework. We show how senior leaders can work together to allocate work assignments with the conscious intent of developing leaders, thus turning your Plan A into action. The key players in this effort, as the chapter explains, are the line managers who serve as the organization's "talent champions"—people who recognize the vital importance of leadership development and effectively develop their direct reports. They are the tip of the Plan A spear, and we offer advice on how to build more line managers into talent champions by focusing on the "strivers"—the line managers who are eager to develop their people but lack the knack for doing so.

- **Chapter 4—Hiring Externally to Fill Gaps.** One of the goals of developing a Plan A is to help nonprofits reduce their reliance on external hiring to fill leadership gaps. But even the best-prepared organization can't always develop all the future leaders it needs through internal development alone. The problem is, external hiring can be risky. Does your outside candidate fit comfortably in your organization's culture? Does she share your passion for the organization's mission? Drawing upon Bridgespan's past experience providing executive search support to more than 200 nonprofit organizations, this chapter focuses on what you can do to ensure that your search leads you to a candidate who meets your leadership priorities and is set up for success upon arrival. We focus on the importance of working with senior leaders, department heads, and key employees to reach alignment on job descriptions and candidate qualifications, and offer examples of organizations that successfully on-board new hires to ensure they're ready to start contributing on Day One.

- **Chapter 5—Monitoring and Improving Practices.** Of all the leadership development activities covered in this guide, measuring, monitoring, and improving practices is the one nonprofits appear to find most difficult to consistently implement. In this chapter, we discuss why measuring and monitoring your leadership development effort is so important—how else will you learn whether your efforts are working? Moreover, these activities demonstrate the organization's commitment to meeting its leadership development goals and signal to the board, the senior team, and indeed the organization as a whole that they are accountable for meeting those goals. At the same time, we offer advice on what to measure and how. In addition to holding people accountable for implementing the actions required to achieve your Plan A, collecting data allows you to learn what is not working and make course corrections. What's more, measuring and monitoring can shine a spotlight on what is working, so that you can apply those approaches elsewhere in the organization.

- **Chapter 6—Getting Started and Moving Forward.** Once you have read the guide, you may find yourself wondering where to start or how to move forward. In this chapter we summarize some of our key observations and suggest some priorities that should serve both early-stage and more advanced organizations well. In addition, you'll find in each chapter a brief sidebar offering suggestions on how to get started on each of the five core processes covered in the guide.

# What This Guide Is—and Isn't

This guide is designed to be used first and foremost by CEOs or EDs of nonprofit organizations, as well as their senior leadership teams. It presupposes that you have some of the basic human resource building blocks in place. Because the processes we describe all build on and link to your organization's existing human resources practices, we assume that even if your organization does not have a stand-alone human resources function, it has in place a set of job descriptions, performance evaluation processes, and systems for recruiting and compensation. If your organization is like most nonprofits (and most for-profit businesses, for that matter) those practices are likely to need some fine-tuning, but you can build on them even if they're imperfect.

This guide is for organizations seeking to adopt ongoing leadership development processes, not for organizations facing an imminent succession challenge, particularly of the CEO. Indeed, the intent is to help organizations avoid that situation by formulating their overarching Plan A. However, if you and your organization urgently need to bring a new leader on board, we have included several helpful reference works in the list of additional resources beginning on page 164.

Nowhere do we attempt to define what makes a good leader or describe the competencies and characteristics that any leader must have. In fact, this guide emphasizes that good leaders are as varied as the organizations they lead, and that it's up to you to decide what competencies and characteristics are right for your organization. Moreover, what your organization needs today might not be what it needs tomorrow. That's one of the most important things you can learn by preparing your Plan A.

# Partners on Our Research Journey

The advice and suggestions in this guide come from four primary sources. These sources include our own study of practices employed by nonprofit networks of different sizes in different fields; many have hundreds of affiliates whose budgets range from less than $1 million to more than $100 million. We interviewed senior leaders of these networks in depth to learn how they and their affiliates approached the Plan A challenge in a considered, methodical way. A second source comprises input from more than 907 direct service nonprofit leaders who have responded to Bridgespan's Leadership Development Diagnostic Survey. Their candid comments deepened our understanding of the state of nonprofit leadership development today and gave us a strong sense of the practices that organizations find most challenging. Third, we reviewed outside studies and writings on leadership development and succession planning, including classics like Tom Adams' *The Nonprofit Leadership Transition and Development Guide* and Ram Charan's *The Leadership Pipeline* (for more titles, see the bibliography of leadership development literature on page 164). Finally, we calibrated our findings against the best practices of the for-profit sector, as compiled by the CEB's Corporate Leadership Council; in many cases we found best corporate practices helpful for all organizations. We cite the information we gathered from all these sources throughout the guide. (You can find a full list of sources and contributors beginning on page 149.)

Our research journey is by no means complete—in fact, we are likely closer to the beginning than the end. As you read the guide and begin to implement new practices within your organization, we hope you will share your experiences with us and visit us at the Plan A section of the Bridgespan website (www.bridgespan.org/Leadership-Development-Tools), where we will be collecting the tools and resources we receive on an ongoing basis.

# Chapter 1: Engaging Your Senior Leaders

*You don't feel nervous, exactly. As CEO of your nonprofit, you've led high-stakes meetings before. But you're aware of a strong sense of urgency. There's a lot riding on today's conversation—nothing less than your organization's future. Over the past several weeks, you and your senior leadership team have been mapping out a strategy for the next three years, one that includes adding several new sites and under-taking a handful of exciting new initiatives. And as you've thought about executing this plan, you've realized that you can't get from here to there without a corps of new leaders, with skills and experiences that leaders in your organization haven't needed to call on before. You also need them to take over some of the tasks you've traditionally done so that you can refocus on several new strategic priorities.*

*Today, you'll be asking your team to join you on a journey into unfamiliar territory—launching an effort to beef up the organization's leadership development capabilities. You'll be requiring a lot of them, and of yourself. Most of your team is new to the work of leadership development, and you're not completely sure you know how to help them. Can you count on your senior leadership team for effective support of your efforts? Are your team members equipped to mentor your high-potential leadership candidates, and if not, can you round up coaches who can sharpen their skills? Do you have the budgetary resources to support such an ambitious agenda?*

*Do you have any choice? To deliver on the strategy you and your team have set for yourselves, you are going to have to develop a cadre of new leaders from within the organization. The question for tonight is how do you make your pitch that developing future leaders, successors even, must become a key part of every leader's job? With everyone stretched thin already, how can you make the best possible case that the mission depends on investing in this way? And how can you be sure your team not only commits but backs its commitment with credible action? With the few minutes remaining before the meeting begins, you look over your notes one last time...*

Ask any expert on leadership, and you'll probably get the same answer: The leader of any group—large or small, a nonprofit or a for-profit company, a soccer team or a rock band—sets the organization's tone and directs its focus. That's why it is essential that leadership development initiatives at nonprofits begin at the very top, with the CEO.

In our interviews with nonprofit leaders, including CEOs and senior human resources (HR) professionals, the message we heard was consistent: When it comes to leadership development and succession planning, the CEO leads the way. Regardless of titles, the CEO is the chief talent officer. No one else can more effectively champion the cause, and development efforts will make little headway if the CEO is unsupportive. But no CEO can do it alone. To build the next generation of leaders, the CEO needs to influence the work and perspective of everyone else involved in the effort, most importantly senior leaders and the board. Above all, the CEO needs to visibly lead the creation of the organization's Plan A, its road map for developing the leaders who can advance the organization's mission.

This chapter explores how CEOs can do that job effectively. We have identified five action steps where the CEO's investment of time and energy can deliver outsize returns. In this chapter we will discuss how nonprofit CEOs can:

- Step 1: Make it clear that leadership development is a strategic priority.
- Step 2: Set expectations for senior leaders and hold them accountable.

- Step 3: Build and develop the senior team.

- Step 4: Make the most of your HR resources.

- Step 5: Engage the board regularly.

How well are nonprofit CEOs currently performing these crucial tasks? According to our Leadership Development Diagnostic Survey, the results are mixed. Seventy-six percent of respondents report that the CEO is actively engaged in building a strong pipeline of leadership candidates. But approximately 60 percent also say that senior leaders aren't held accountable for their development efforts and that organizations aren't investing sufficient resources into leadership development. If those scores are any guide—and we believe they are—many well-intentioned CEOs are not yet doing enough to build a strong leadership pipeline. We hope that this chapter and the rest of the guide will help CEOs and their organizations close this gap between intention and action.

## Are Your Senior Leaders Engaged? An Excerpt from Our Leadership Development Diagnostic Survey

Are the following statements true of your organization?

- The CEO/executive director is actively engaged in building a strong pipeline of future leaders.

- Current leaders are actively engaged in building a strong pipeline of future leaders.

- Board members are appropriately engaged in building a strong pipeline of future leaders.

- Current leaders are equipped to develop future leaders.

- Current leaders are held accountable for building a strong pipeline of future leaders.
- Current leaders are recognized for their efforts to develop future leaders.
- Organizational culture supports and values leadership development.
- Sufficient resources (e.g., funding, time) are invested in leadership development.

# Step 1: Make It Clear that Leadership Development Is a Strategic Priority

CEOs, nonprofit and for-profit alike, like to say that "our people are our most important asset." And they frequently stress the value of "getting the right people on the bus," in Jim Collins' words.[4] But it's far less common to hear a CEO draw a clear connection between the presence of effective leaders and the organization's ability to make an impact. When CEOs do make that connection, the statement resonates. CEOs who make a clear business case for leadership development are often able to win over the skeptics (and there are always a few) who view people development as secondary to their "real work."

### Link Leadership Development to Superior Performance

How do leaders make this case? One approach is to produce evidence that leadership development leads to stronger results. Roxanne Spillett, former CEO of Boys and Girls Clubs of America (BGCA) did just that. Although the method she chose is likely to be too costly and time-consuming for

---

4 Jim Collins. *Good to Great: Why Some Companies Make the Leap... and Others Don't* (William Collins, 2001).

many nonprofits to contemplate, leaders of other nonprofits can reference the results of her effort without necessarily duplicating it. And, as we'll see, the results are well worth referencing.

At Spillett's behest, BGCA engaged management consultancy McKinsey & Co. to perform a study of leadership training. An article in the July 2010 issue of *McKinsey Quarterly*[5] describes how the consulting team systematically studied nearly 50 aspects of leadership at BGCA and isolated four—the leader's ability to build an effective board, find and pursue effective revenue-development strategies, bring an investor's mindset to programs and resource development, and lead with tenacity and persistence—that had an outsize impact on organizational performance. BGCA then worked with more than 1,000 leaders from more than 400 local affiliates to develop those leadership traits.

BGCA compared the performance of local affiliates whose leaders had gone through the program against a control group made up of affiliates whose leaders had not yet participated in the program. BGCA learned that the affiliates whose leaders had undergone training outperformed the control group in fundraising, enrollment in Club membership and program participation, and retention of young people. It also learned that the training program generated financial returns that were more than four times its cost. These findings, which are cited in the *McKinsey Quarterly* article, are tremendously persuasive, according to Jeff Amy, BGCA's vice president for training and professional development. "The leadership training costs affiliates more in terms of time and money than anything they've done with BGCA before," Amy said. "The results from the McKinsey article are one of the most powerful arguments that the investment is worthwhile."

---

5 "Putting a Value on Training," *McKinsey Quarterly*, July 2010.

## Link Leadership to Strategy

Another way for leaders to make the business case for leadership development is to draw a clear connection between strategic priorities and leadership needs. Whether your organization aims to expand programs, open new sites, replace retiring leaders, or adapt to changing external contexts, it needs the right leaders—"the right people on the bus"—to get the job done. At the KIPP Foundation, one of the largest operators of charter schools in the United States, CEO Richard Barth and his senior team are stressing leadership development to meet the organization's ambitious goals for growth. With 109 schools and 32,000 students in its network, the organization is aiming to expand to more than 55,000 students by 2015, while continuing to deliver the high-quality education for which KIPP is known. KIPP can only get there, Barth and his senior team tell the organization, if it has the right leaders in place. It's a powerful message made all the more powerful because the messenger is often Barth himself.

Pam Moeller, a consultant with the KIPP Foundation, says the message is getting through. At the organization's schools, the challenge of maintaining quality during a period of rapid growth has brought KIPP "to the place where leaders see that their primary job is developing other leaders," she said. "You start to look at our growth aspirations and the reality of the numbers, and once you look at those facts, you realize that developing leaders is important."

By making a clear link between effective leaders and organizational outcomes, Richard Barth at KIPP and Roxanne Spillett at BGCA are driving home the message that leadership development is instrumental to fulfilling their organizations' missions. That's an argument that resonates with their listeners who, after all, signed on because they're committed to those missions. Linking leadership to the mission is a highly effective way to prove that leadership development, far from being ancillary to an organization's real work, is integral to it. From there, it's just a short step to asking the organization's other leaders to commit themselves to leadership development—and demanding that they show results.

# Step 2: Set Expectations for Senior Leaders and Hold Them Accountable

The CEO states the vision and makes the case for leadership development, but it's senior leaders who are responsible for executing the development strategy and cascading it down by example to other managers in the organization. Since the majority of leadership development occurs on the job (something discussed in detail later in this guide), it's up to the senior leaders to provide growth opportunities to their direct reports and coach them through the process. They are also responsible for drawing up a Plan A for their departments, in which they lay out their plans for developing their teams to meet the leadership challenges of the next three years.

Setting the expectation that senior leaders will take on these responsibilities and fulfill them successfully, and that they will push this down to other managers within their organizations, starts with setting the right expectations for what it means to be a manager at any level.

### Tie Leadership Development to Job Descriptions and Promotions

When it comes to leadership development, the Y-USA, whose more than 2,600 Y's are dedicated to strengthening the communities they serve, leaves no room for doubt in the minds of its people. For starters, all staff members are considered leaders—even newcomers understand that leadership is an integral part of their work. And Y-USA's leadership competency development guide states explicitly that the staff who seek to progress in their Y careers, advancing from "leader" to "team leader" to "multi-team or branch leader" to "organizational leader," are expected to assume increasing responsibility for developing others. Leaders are expected to share their experiences with co-workers and help train them to do their jobs. So are team leaders, but they're also asked to go a step further and actively participate in recruiting to ensure that new hires are assigned to roles appropriate to their abilities. Multi-team or branch leaders, too, are expected to participate in training and recruiting, but they're also expected to take on additional responsibility for identifying performance gaps, shaping development plans, and developing the coaching and mentoring skills of their direct reports. In other words, each upward move in the organization is accompanied by broader and deeper developmental responsibilities, and this is true across all 18 leadership competencies. (See the graphic on the next page for details on the "Developing Others" leadership competency at the Y.)

## Make Leadership Development a Goal in Senior Leaders' Performance Reviews

Another effective way to reinforce the importance of leadership development is for the CEO to ask senior leaders to set specific goals for developing future leaders in their departments and hold them accountable for attaining them by incorporating the goals into their performance evaluations. That's what Carolyn Miles did when she took the reins at Save the Children, a global nonprofit devoted to making breakthroughs in the way the world treats children and creating lasting, positive changes in their lives. She was chief operating officer (COO) and became president and CEO after a time when employee frustration with the organization's career planning and developmental efforts was high. Staff engagement surveys had shown a clear need

# Developing Others at the Y: Competency description

| BEHAVIOR DESCRIPTION | | | |
|---|---|---|---|
| **Leader** | **Team Leader** | **Multi-Team or Branch Leader** | **Organizational Leader** |
| • Shares experiences and provides training to assist others with their development.<br><br>• Proactively shares information, advice, and suggestions to help others be more successful.<br><br>• Provides constructive, behaviorally specific feedback to others. | • Ensures appropriate fit when recruiting and hiring.<br><br>• Continually assesses the skills and abilities of others to identify developmental opportunities.<br><br>• Coaches others in creating and implementing their development plans.<br><br>• Is capable of delivering positive and constructive feedback to motivate, encourage, and support others in their development.<br><br>• Provides staff with the time, tools, and resources necessary to meet or exceed job requirements.<br><br>**+**<br><br>Leader behaviors | • Analyzes performance gaps and builds plans to develop the abilities of others to perform and contribute to the organization.<br><br>• Provides ongoing feedback and opportunities to learn through formal and informal methods.<br><br>• Holds managers accountable for staff development.<br><br>• Develops direct reports' mentoring and coaching skills.<br><br>• Guides others on how to strengthen knowledge, skills, and competencies that improve organizational performance.<br><br>**+**<br><br>Leader & Team Leader behaviors | • Creates a development-focused culture by speaking regularly with people at all levels in the organization about their development plans.<br><br>• Promotes the importance of recruiting, hiring, and managing the talents of staff and volunteers.<br><br>• Engages in and champions ongoing feedback, coaching, and opportunities for informal and formal learning at all levels.<br><br>**+**<br><br>Leader, Team Leader, & Multi-Team or Branch Leader behaviors |

Source: Developing Cause-Driven Leadership®, Leadership Competency Development Guide, YMCA of the USA

to continue to improve development practices, and some talented staff and leaders had left.

Recognizing the need to retain key staff and groom them for greater responsibility, Miles, as COO, had communicated both formally and informally to her senior leadership team and other managers that they would be held accountable for developing their direct reports. She spelled out her expectations in a memo circulated throughout the organization. Crucially, she backed up her words with enhancements to Save the Children's existing HR processes. She used goal-setting sessions, performance evaluations, and formal check-ins with her direct reports to highlight the importance of leadership development. She asked each member of the leadership team to identify five or six objectives for the year, and one of the objectives had to be tied to talent and leadership development. Miles also built follow-up into the process, scheduling twice-yearly conversations with each team member, separate from performance reviews, to discuss progress toward development goals (see the sidebar on page 34 for details on Save the Children's development calendar). In doing so, she modeled the behavior she expected from her team members, making clear that she expected them to have similar conversations with their direct reports.

Drawing on her private-sector experience, Miles, as COO, also had initiated a succession-planning process with her direct reports and their direct reports. For the first time, senior leaders were asked to formally assess the performance and potential of their direct reports and identify the people who would be ready to step immediately into a greater leadership role, as well as the people who would be ready after additional development. (More on assessing the potential of staff can be found later in this guide.)

The succession-planning exercise quickly took root with some, but not all, senior team leaders. It soon became apparent that several members of the team took their development responsibility seriously, while others looked on it as a perfunctory exercise, a bureaucratic box to be checked off. Working with the HR team, Miles ensured the process was shared across the senior team with a meeting during which senior leaders openly discussed succession candidates. Miles impressed upon them the importance of leadership development and together, with the HR team, coached them in the techniques and skills they could employ to make their people better leaders. Now as CEO, Miles has added an annual review of top spot succession plans with the board to bring them into the mix.

The process has taken many senior team members out of their comfort zones. "In general," Miles told us, "our culture is more about equality than about differentiation." It was a new experience to be asked to single out some individuals as having greater leadership potential than others. And some senior leaders had trouble with the emotional challenges that can arise during development conversations with their direct reports. Despite the difficulties, Miles persuaded her team to buy into the process by repeatedly making the connection between Save the Children's mission and the need for leadership development and using HR processes to amplify the message. There's a lesson here for every nonprofit. By definition they are mission-driven organizations. Like Barth, Miles, and Spillett, CEOs must make the case that developing leaders gives their organizations a better chance to fulfill those missions. Getting there means leveraging the organization's HR processes to establish leadership development as an organizational priority.

# Senior Engagement at Save the Children: Conversation Calendar

Save the Children's CEO Carolyn Miles makes sure that timely leadership development discussions occur with her senior reports by scheduling them.

**December:** CEO meets with each member of the senior team to set five or six individual goals for the coming year. At least one of those goals must be related to leadership development. Team members know they will be evaluated on their progress against those goals.

**January:** CEO holds talent-review meetings with each member of the senior team. Team members assess the succession potential of each of their direct reports, identifying people who are ready to step immediately into a greater leadership role and those who will be ready after future development. Data gathered during these meetings feeds into the CEO's annual report to the board on talent and leadership development, delivered at the end of the first quarter.

**February:** Review of succession plan for senior team with the board and vice president of human resources in closed-door session.

**March, September:** CEO holds progress meetings with individual team members, checking on their progression against goals. Senior team members are expected to conduct similar meetings with their direct reports.

**October:** CEO meets with the entire senior leadership team to review and update organization's succession plan.

# Step 3: Build and Develop the Senior Team

As Carolyn Miles' example illustrates, the CEO's work with the organization's senior team is a powerful way to signal the value of leadership development throughout the organization. By asking her senior leaders to include a personal-development goal in their five or six annual goals, and by making clear she expects them to ask the same of their direct reports, the CEO can generate organizational momentum for leadership development. She can sustain the momentum by checking in periodically with her team members to assess their progress against their individual goals, and by making clear she expects them to hold similar check-ins with their direct reports. And she can reinforce the all-in-a-day's-work aspect of leadership development by incorporating these conversations into the organization's preexisting processes.

Above all, she can help leadership development go viral in the organization by working with senior team members to create a Plan A for their areas of responsibility. These plans include a vision for how the team may need to evolve to tackle new priorities and address critical competency gaps. The plans take into account the skills and aspirations of the individual team members themselves, some of whom may be eager to ramp up their careers, while others may be looking to wind down their work or retire. Ultimately, each department's Plan A can be consolidated into a master Plan A, an organizational road map for development that offers opportunities for leaders to evolve in a manner that suits both their aspirations and the organization's broader development needs.

To reiterate: The nonprofit leaders we spoke with repeatedly stress that the CEO needs to get the ball rolling by working on the senior leadership team's own development. After that, it's the job of senior team members to do the same with their direct reports. It's critical that this type of planning start at the top. "This has to be owned by the CEO," said Rod Davis, Save the Children's former vice president for human resources.

## Questions the CEO Should Ask Each Senior Team Member about Leadership Development

- What do you think the leadership team of your department/division is going to look like in three years?

- Do you think we have the internal talent you will need to execute over the next three years? For which positions are we likely to need to look externally?

- Do you talk to your direct reports about their aspirations and development needs and incorporate these in their development plans? Are they doing the same with the staff they manage?

- What actions are you taking to develop your direct reports? Where do you need help?

- Is there anything that's working particularly well—and that we should share with the rest of the senior team?

- What are you doing to develop yourself?

## Step 4: Make the Most of Your HR Resources

Many nonprofit organizations are too small to have a formal HR staff. Those that do have the staff can help themselves by clarifying the important supporting role that HR can play in leadership development efforts. It's a role that may evolve as the organization's HR capabilities grow. For example, organizations whose HR capabilities are limited primarily to administrative tasks like payroll and benefits processing might ask an HR staff member simply to collect data for decision making and ensure that senior leaders are following up on their responsibilities. As the organization grows and the HR function becomes more robust, HR can provide simple development tools and frameworks, and act as a clearinghouse for Plan A information. It can also begin to integrate development-related processes into existing workflows wherever possible. HR can start by incorporating development metrics into annual reviews, for example, or by scheduling regular feedback sessions where managers review development progress with their direct reports.

Organizations with strong HR functions can use HR leaders to coach, counsel, and advise line managers with little or no experience in talent development. Senior HR leaders with a thorough understanding of the organization's mission and core competencies can also serve as strategic thought partners to the CEO and the senior leadership team. In this role they need to be both demanding and supportive, asking tough human capital–related questions. Among such probing queries are: Is this senior leader realistically assessing her department's future needs? Is she overstating or understating their potential? This is all part of the intent to ensure that senior leaders produce rigorous, well-crafted development plans.

## Shared Accountability

The CEOs we've spoken with caution that even the best-intentioned managers can be tempted to delegate their roles to HR. And so they make a point of reminding senior leaders that it's their job, not HR's, to deliver tough messages and address competency shortfalls in their direct reports. The bottom line: HR is a partner in leadership development and shares responsibility for its results. Ultimately, though, senior leaders have to own the process.

# Step 5: Engage the Board Regularly

The board is ultimately accountable for the organization's success and, with the CEO, shares responsibility for ensuring that it has the leadership necessary to pursue its mission consistently and effectively over time. At present, though, 57 percent of respondents to our Leadership Development Diagnostic Survey either disagree or strongly disagree that their boards are appropriately engaged in developing the leadership pipeline. Anecdotal evidence suggests, in fact, that many boards consider the topic of leadership development and succession planning only when the time comes to select the next CEO. Once a successor is chosen and the selection committee disbands, the board turns its attention to other matters—until the next succession crisis erupts. By taking up the role of chief talent officer, CEOs can break this pattern and make leadership development and succession planning an integral part of the board's work.

Experienced CEOs and board leaders highlight four ways to effectively partner in leadership development. These activities not only support CEO succession but also contribute to a healthy leadership pipeline at every level of the organization. These activities include:

- Developing the CEO and ensuring that she has potential successors and a Plan A in place for the CEO role;

- Holding the CEO accountable for developing senior leaders and ensuring that members of the senior team have a Plan A in place for their positions;

- With the CEO, supporting the development of future leaders by integrating leadership development within core processes of the organization, particularly those where the board is engaged (e.g., annual budgeting, strategic planning); and

- With the CEO, agreeing on leadership development goals for the organization and monitoring progress against them.

## Developing the CEO

The board's job begins with delivering regular, formal performance reviews of the CEO. While this may seem like an obvious step, BoardSource's most recent survey of board practices found that approximately 30 percent of EDs had not received a review from their board in the previous 12 months.[6] This represents a missed opportunity to hold the CEO accountable for her job performance—including, crucially, her own development as a leader.

The most effective nonprofit boards review the CEO's performance at least annually. They help her identify her own professional development goals and craft a plan for making progress against them.

Just as important, the board evaluates the CEO's success in developing others, including possible successors. That means that board members need to press the issue, if necessary, with the CEO. The sidebar "Questions the Board Should Ask the CEO about Leadership Development" on page 45 suggests some questions that board members should regularly ask the CEO. By emphasizing leadership development in the CEO's evaluation, the board signals to the CEO that it sees it as a strategic priority and that it expects the CEO to do so as well—in part by taking the steps, such as senior leader development, highlighted early in this chapter.

By promoting and supporting the CEO's own development and her development work with her leadership team, the board also sends a signal that resonates throughout the organization. Simply put, when the board makes leadership development a priority for the CEO, the CEO is more likely to make it a priority for everyone else. And by placing leadership development within the CEO's performance expectations, the board gives the CEO a strong incentive

---

6 BoardSource Nonprofit Governance Index 2010.

to seek the support needed for her leadership development work to succeed. That support might include work with a mentor or coach to strengthen her performance as a "talent champion"—a manager who both recognizes the importance of developing talent and is effective in doing so.[7]

### Holding the CEO and Senior Leaders Accountable for Identifying Likely Successors and Developing These Future Leaders

Among the paramount responsibilities of any nonprofit board is ensuring orderly leadership transitions, even if the CEO or another senior leader departs suddenly. Yet nonprofit leaders give themselves low marks for such preparation. According to our Leadership Development Diagnostic Survey, 59 percent of respondents disagreed or strongly disagreed with the statement that "we have identified successors for crucial positions."

The Plan A process offers boards the opportunity to fulfill, at least in part, their succession-related responsibilities. That's not to say that the board should regularly engage in the appointment of senior leaders other than the CEO. There may be a few instances where the board has significant interaction with leaders and may provide input to the CEO on the selection of her direct reports. For example, the board's audit committee might be asked to provide input on the appointment or hiring of the chief financial officer (CFO). But when it comes to leadership development, the board's primary job is to hold the CEO accountable for creating a Plan A that anticipates the organization's future needs, and to see to it that CEO engages the senior team fully in the leadership development effort.

---

7  Corporate Leadership Council Human Resources, *Corporate Leadership Council Talent Management Effectiveness Survey*.

That means holding the CEO accountable for ensuring that her senior team has a Plan A in place for each of their roles. Have the CEO and senior team identified potential successors, both short-term and long-term, to fill key roles? Have they assessed these successors, documented gaps in their development, and formulated a set of work opportunities and formal learning to address those gaps? Have they made provisions for new or expanded leadership roles? Have they set a timeline for the development of each possible successor and senior leadership candidate? These are the key elements of any leadership-development plan, and, as we will see later, form the basis for the benchmarks for measuring the plan's progress.

By reviewing the organization's Plan A with the CEO, the board also gives the CEO the opportunity to seek the board's support in fulfilling the plan. That support might take the form of financial resources (for activities such as recruiting or professional-development courses) or advisory resources (such as engaging·a consultant to lead a workshop on constructive performance reviews, for example, or to facilitate an offsite devoted to evaluating staffers' leadership potential).

Aside from emphasizing the CEO's responsibility to work with her team to create a Plan A, boards can support leadership development by inviting interactions with emerging leaders. When leadership candidates undertake tasks such as delivering presentations to the board, they not only get the opportunity to develop on the job, they also have a chance to develop important relationships with board members who can serve as informal role models or mentors (not as managers, though— that's the CEO's job). At the same time, board members get a chance to assess the leadership abilities of potential internal candidates for senior positions. Such activities can only help the board fulfill two of its most crucial roles: preparing the organization for leadership transitions and ensuring that the organization has an active pipeline of future leaders.

## Integrating Leadership Development into Core Organizational Processes

As we've noted elsewhere, organizations that effectively develop future leaders incorporate leadership development into the rhythms of their everyday work. For boards this means embedding leadership development into core governance processes such as budgeting, planning, and progress reviews. Viewing these processes as a means of promoting leadership development (among other things) goes a long way toward instilling a leadership development mindset at the highest levels of the organization—a mindset that views leadership development as critical to the organization's mission and that adjusts its leadership development work to keep pace with changes in the organization's strategy and ways of doing business.

Simply by taking leadership development into account during the crucial tasks of annual planning and budgeting, the board elevates leadership development to the same plane as other key organizational activities. Including leadership development in the budget process helps focus the organization on allocating resources to support development. And resource allocation in itself signals to the organization that leadership development isn't just this year's fashionable trend—it's an investment in the organization's future. (On page 45, "How the Girl Scouts' Board Supports Leadership Development" describes how the board of one large national organization integrated leadership development into its core processes.)

Including leadership development as part of broader strategic planning, meanwhile, enables the board to revisit leadership development needs periodically and make course corrections in light of changes in strategic priorities. Such reviews give the board an opportunity to align leadership development with anticipated changes in the organization. After all, a well-crafted Plan A, at least in its early iterations, is a vision of the organization's senior roles needed three to five years in the future (later iterations of Plan A take lower-level roles into account as well). As strategy shifts, those needs are likely to shift as well, affecting the organization's leadership development priorities and activities. By revisiting the organization's Plan A during the course of strategic planning, boards and senior leaders can anticipate how roles might expand, contract, or be added as changes occur. Armed with that insight, the board (as well as the CEO and senior leaders responsible for crafting the organization's Plan A) can act ahead of time to invest in the development of high-potential individuals within the organization or plan for recruiting outside the organization to fill those leadership gaps.

## Setting Leadership Development Goals and Monitoring Progress

One of the key ways that boards establish accountability is by monitoring and measuring progress against goals. For example, many boards have metrics to give them quick reads on progress against fundraising and membership goals, or to measure the effectiveness of service offerings to the community the nonprofit serves. Yet few boards have integrated metrics that allow them to monitor leadership development goals—a significant oversight, given the vital importance of leadership development to the organization's impact.

Identifying the right set of measures or milestones to monitor doesn't just help the board do its job better—it also helps the CEO with her job. Larger organizations might want to focus first on measuring how healthy the pipeline is for key roles. For example, a relevant measure for the health of a charter school network's pipeline might regard be number of assistant principals ready to step up to principal roles if needed. Smaller organizations might find it more useful to conduct a more qualitative review of how a few key leaders are progressing in their own development.

While the specific metrics will change from one organization to the next, they all serve the same purpose: to enable the board to measure progress against the leadership development goals. We recommend that the board make check-ins on the status of the leadership development a recurring item on the board calendar. A logical time is during annual planning meetings, when the board can review the organization's leadership and talent management road map in addition to reviewing other plans and budgets. Given the sensitivity of the topic, many organizations will want to conduct these discussions during executive sessions. But the check-ins will provide the board with a high-level view of the progress of leadership development activities. The board can then work with the CEO to improve the effectiveness of those activities.

At the same time, metrics and milestones help boards avoid the temptation to micromanage. With the board focused on the big picture—looking at overall progress against high-level goals—the CEO and her senior team are free to test various approaches to meeting those goals. If one approach isn't working, the lack of progress will show up soon enough on the metrics, and the CEO and her team can make adjustments. The board need intervene only when results deviate sharply— whether positively or negatively—from the norm.

For more on the role of the board in supporting leadership development, see Bridgespan's diagnostic tool for boards in the Appendix.

# Questions the Board Should Ask the CEO about Leadership Development

- What is your senior leadership team going to look like in three years?
- Do you have the internal talent you need to execute our strategic priorities over the next three years? For which positions are we likely to need to look externally?
- What are you doing to develop internal talent?
- Who are the rising stars that we should meet?
- What are you doing to develop yourself?
- What can we do to help you with your development or development of your staff?

### How the Girl Scouts' Board Supports Leadership Development

One board that has made significant contributions to leadership development is the national board of the Girl Scouts of the United States of America (GSUSA). In fact, the board has done everything that CEOs and other leadership development experts recommend a board should do—developing the CEO; holding the CEO accountable for developing her senior team; integrating leadership development within core processes of the organization and board; and tracking progress against leadership development goals.

Early in her tenure, CEO Kathy Cloninger, now retired, focused on making GSUSA an even more effective organization. One of the first things she did was to work with the national board to restructure the organization's governance model. The board dissolved its Human Resources Committee and replaced it with an Executive Compensation Committee that was focused initially on reviewing and developing the

# Get the Ball Rolling: Engaging Your Senior Leaders

**Tips for those at an early stage...**

**Add leadership development to the annual goals** of each member of your senior team:

- Require senior leaders to add a personal and an organizational development goal to their list of annual goals.

- Add such goals to your own objectives.

- Use your goal-setting and performance review process to hold your senior team accountable for progress.

- Let them know that you have shared your own goals with the board and that it will hold you accountable for meeting them.

- Encourage the board to monitor and measure leadership development the same way they monitor progress against fundraising, membership, and program goals.

**...and at a more advanced stage**

**Extend the goal-setting process** to the direct reports of the senior team:

- To keep the process manageable, consider focusing initially on a handful of staff members before including the rest in the exercise.

- When everyone at the next level has completed the goal-setting exercise for themselves, ask them to work on identifying development goals with *their* direct reports.

- Ensure that development goal-setting and review becomes embedded at every level of the organization.

CEO. Among those assigned to the committee were newly recruited board members with extensive experience in corporate HR. They brought a new emphasis on leadership development to the board and encouraged their colleagues to become more actively engaged in planning annual goals with Cloninger. To emphasize that leadership development was a priority, the board required Cloninger each year to include a goal related to developing her senior team and planning for succession.

The Executive Compensation Committee started meeting every two months. Rather than dwell on the narrow question of the CEO's development, committee members also began to consider how senior team members were being reviewed and developed—precisely the shift in focus that leadership development dashboards can promote. Drawing on corporate experience, several new board members repeatedly raised questions about the organization's bench depth. They urged the rest of the board to hold the senior team accountable for developing leaders, not just for hitting operational or program goals. In this respect, the GSUSA board parted company with many other nonprofit boards whose purview is limited to the CEO's performance.

The committee did more than just ask a lot of questions. It developed a formal process for reviewing potential successors and the organization's plans for preparing them for greater responsibility. Although the board's mandate was limited to the senior leadership team, the succession planning process has cascaded down through the organization. GSUSA's management staff now routinely plans for succession and development, identifying close to 100 potential successors for top management roles. A chief learning officer, recruited from the corporate world for her extensive experience in leadership development, actively supports the management staff's planning efforts.

Committee members also started working with Cloninger to think about rising stars among their council leaders (that is, leaders of local affiliates). This work led to a more formal process of creating a watch list of council leaders and a strategy to assign them to national task forces to give them exposure and determine their interest in greater leadership. Among the rising stars on the watch list was Cloninger's eventual successor as CEO, Anna Maria Chavez.

# Fostering a Culture of Leadership Development

"Culture" can be a squishy term, but it is simply how things get done—the norms and accepted rules of engagement that govern how staff members conduct themselves, interact with one another, and interact with the people they serve. No staff member has more influence over the norms of an organization than the CEO. That's why we have stressed in this chapter and indeed throughout this guide that the CEO bears the most responsibility for fostering a culture of leadership development.

CEOs build culture through their patterns of communication and personal action. What CEOs choose to do and not do, where they invest their time, energy, and attention, sends strong signals about what they value. We strongly encourage CEOs, therefore, not just to work on developing their direct reports, but also to engage strategically and visibly in broad development efforts. That might mean cultivating relationships with high-potential leadership candidates, or it might mean building up leadership pipelines for critical roles. By making these activities highly visible, CEOs send the organization the message that leadership development isn't just a buzz phrase, it's a high priority. Prepared statements and pep talks won't get the job done. The CEO's actions speak louder than words.

### Reading, Writing, and Revitalization at Youth Villages

Patrick Lawler demonstrated his priorities this way when he became CEO of Youth Villages, a national leader in offering services to disadvantaged and emotionally troubled young people. The organization faced a broad set of challenges when he stepped into the role, and he wasn't sure how to tackle them. Spurred by an offhand suggestion by a colleague in the field, he became a voracious reader of business books, using the knowledge to propose several initiatives that have revitalized the organization. "Every book I've read has had some impact on what we do at Youth Villages," he told us.

He started by sharing what he was reading in his monthly emails to the staff. Next, he posted a recommended reading list on the Youth Villages intranet (he updates the list frequently). Today, quarterly staff meetings feature a table at the back of the room where Lawler places a few books that have a bearing on issues that will be raised during the meeting. He'll refer to some in the course of the meeting, holding them up and quoting or paraphrasing pertinent passages. Lawler encourages managers to read the books and share their lessons with their staff, offering prizes and rewards, such as merchandise from the Youth Villages store, to managers who post reviews of the books in the organization's intranet. (For a list of Lawler's "must reads" for nonprofit leaders, please see "A Good Book's Role in Professional Development" on www.bridgespan.org.)

The reading lists and book reviews are, of course, just one of the ways that Lawler is instilling a culture of learning and leadership development at Youth Village. But his methods resonate throughout the organization because they are a visible, tangible expression of Lawler's authentic enthusiasm and his commitment to learning, reflection, and growth. "Reading and writing," he said, "help you work through things more than you're able to going through the day." By signaling what he values, Lawler has encouraged the organization to value books and learning. And because many of Lawler's favorite books deal extensively with leadership development and succession planning, they provide a natural opening for Lawler to raise those topics at quarterly management meetings.

# The Rest of the Story

*That went pretty well, you think to yourself. The conversation hit most of the high points. That* McKinsey Quarterly *article certainly didn't hurt. You could see several members of the team were intrigued when you put up the slide summarizing the research findings. It went a long way toward making the case for leadership development by linking it to the strategic goals you've been discussing for the last several months. And by acknowledging that you, as CEO, are the chief talent officer for the organization, you signaled your personal commitment to leadership development. The rest of the senior team was more ready to climb aboard after you discussed the potential upside of building an organization that could meet its leadership needs consistently over time. And if you do say so yourself, you did a pretty good job of making clear that you would set expectations for the effort and hold everyone accountable, beginning with yourself.*

*It's just a start, you think. But it's a good one.*

# Chapter 2: Understanding Your Future Needs

*Maybe that was the easy part, you think to yourself. I made my pitch for engaging more deeply in leadership development, and the senior leadership team signed on, unanimously and, for the most part, enthusiastically. But now we have to figure out what kind of leaders we need to develop. And we can't decide that without first figuring out what sort of organization we are, and what sort of organization we'll be in three years. Where to begin?*

*Well, it seems logical to begin with the changes we have planned. For the first time in the organization's history, we're going to advocate for new state and federal policy. Our communications director has experience in this field, but we'll need to give some other members of the team exposure to the public policy arena. And with the new sites we hope to open, we're going to need several new site directors. Then there's our head of HR, who's thinking more and more about starting her well-earned retirement. We're going to want to beef up the HR department over time, so her replacement should be someone who has helped other organizations build up their HR functions. Are there people further down in the organization who can fill the gaps? Will they be ready in the next two or three years? I'm going to have to sit down with the leadership team and start to figure this out...*

Robert Ottenhoff would likely sympathize with our hypothetical CEO's concerns. He and the organization he formerly led, GuideStar, faced what he has called "a sobering period" in late 2002. Ottenhoff had just been named president of GuideStar, a nonprofit that gathers and publicizes information about nonprofit organizations, and GuideStar's funding consortium, a group of large philanthropic foundations, took the occasion to deliver a challenge: Until you develop a plan for sustainability, you'll receive no further funding from us.

That got GuideStar's attention. To become self-sustaining, GuideStar had to overhaul its funding and operating model. Instead of supporting its activities with foundation grants and giving away its products and services, GuideStar would need to start charging at least some of its customers. But Ottenhoff and his colleagues realized that if GuideStar was going to charge for some services, it would have to upgrade the quality of those offerings. "When you offer everything for free," Ottenhoff said, "good enough is good enough. But when you are charging a customer, they expect something better."

Ottenhoff and his colleagues concluded that GuideStar needed to develop a team that possessed skills and attitudes more similar to those found in a for-profit business. With those requirements in mind, the organization initiated a review to assess its talent pool and establish expectations for the future. Three key questions guided the review process:

- What is our strategy, and how do we fulfill it?
- What kinds of people do we need to fulfill our strategy?
- How do we develop or find these staff and leaders?

At some point in its existence, every nonprofit arrives at its own "sobering moment." Its leaders realize they must reexamine their goals and assess whether they have the people in place who can lead in the future. What roles will they be asked to fill? Do they have the competencies required to fill those roles? Can those competencies be developed, or will the organization have to look outside to find the next generation of leadership?

These questions take many nonprofits into unfamiliar territory. Only 41 percent of the respondents to our Leadership Development Diagnostic Survey agree or strongly agree that they have "a clear understanding of the leadership capacity (e.g., skills, roles, and number of individuals) our organization will need three to five years from now in order to achieve strategic goals." It's not surprising then that only 41 percent agree or strongly agree that they "have identified potential successors for critical positions" and "where successors are not in place," only 32 percent "have plans in place to address our gaps." As a result, many organizations find themselves caught short when a senior leader departs or a new senior-level position is created. More often than they'd like, they have to hire externally to fill the gap.

It doesn't have to be this way. Some of the nation's most successful nonprofits have shown it's possible to take a systematic approach to understanding future leadership needs. In this chapter, we'll look at the three key steps organizations can take to understand their future needs and prepare to meet them. The steps are general enough that organizations of any size can implement them in some form. The steps call for senior leaders to:

- Step 1: Define the critical leadership capacities needed to fulfill your organization's mission in the next three to five years.

- Step 2: Assess the potential of your staff (current and future leaders) to take on greater responsibility.

- Step 3: Create your Plan A for what leadership teams within the organization will look like in three years.

These steps aren't a one-time event in the life of an organization. It's a good idea to conduct them regularly, although the timing of the steps will vary. The process of defining critical leadership competencies may be repeated every few years, depending on the organization's rate of change, though most nonprofits should revisit their assessment of staff potential and Plan A annually. Let's look at each step in detail, largely through the examples of nonprofits that have gone through the process.

# Do You Understand Your Future Needs? An Excerpt from Our Leadership Development Diagnostic Survey

Are these statements true of your organization?

- The skills required to become a successful leader at various levels of your organization are clear.

- You have an understanding of the leadership capacity (e.g., skills, roles, and number of individuals) your organization will need three to five years from now in order to achieve strategic goals.

- Your employees are systematically evaluated both on their current performance and their potential to move into leadership roles.

- You have identified potential successors for critical positions.

- Where successors are not in place, you have plans in place to address the gaps.

## Step 1: Define the Critical Leadership Capacities Needed to Fulfill Your Organization's Mission in the Next Three to Five Years

Questions about the leadership pipeline have a place in any strategic planning discussion. They are also worth asking at any major organizational inflection point—when the organization is entering a rapid growth phase or consolidating operations, for example, when a senior leader announces plans to retire or depart, or when changes in the external environment require that the organization make changes. Fast-growing organizations especially will want to ask whether they need to add leadership positions or change the scope of existing positions. An organization that's planning to grow by adding new sites, for example, probably needs to develop a cadre of site directors, and possibly a vice president for field operations to support and coordinate site activities. An organization that has shifted its strategy toward greater focus on community engagement may need to enhance the skills of existing or future leaders to work effectively with external stakeholders. These types of shifts may lead the organization to revise the competencies required of future leaders and, consequently, the Plan A for developing the competencies of high-potential individuals.

# Leadership Development Terms Defined

Leadership literature is littered with impressive-sounding buzzwords whose meanings seem to morph with every new usage. Some words seem to be used interchangeably—for example, 99.9 percent of us can't explain the difference between a "skill" and a "competency." Yet the two words mean two different things.

A framework to help clarify the differences among common leadership development terms has been developed by the Corporate Leadership Council (CLC), a unit of CEB, a for-profit business research and advisory service.

According to the CLC, a leader possesses various **competencies** that enable her to do her job. In other words she is "competent" in areas critical for success in her role. Competencies are made up of groups of **behaviors**—the specific actions a leader needs to demonstrate her competence. Someone competent in problem solving, for example, demonstrates a number of behaviors, including the ability to identify and define a problem, break it down into its constituent parts, analyze each part, and develop, test, and implement solutions.

Underpinning these behaviors are skills, knowledge, and traits. **Skills** are learned capacities that enable a person to perform a task. Logical reasoning and presentation delivery are examples of skills. Organizations can often develop such skills in their people through training or by offering appropriate learning opportunities. **Knowledge** is a familiarity with information or facts that can be learned through experiences or education. A leader who displays a firm grasp of healthcare regulations and policies, employment law, or fundraising guidelines demonstrates knowledge. Finally, **traits**—perhaps the least tangible leadership attribute—are the feelings, attitudes, perceptions, and beliefs that a person displays. Traits describe qualities such as curiosity, impartiality, and empathy.

Now let's pull all those terms together, with an example of a nonprofit leader who partners with for-profit insurance companies to deliver a healthcare service. To demonstrate competency at this work, this leader would need certain *skills*—such as the ability to craft and deliver compelling sales pitches to potential insurance partners. To be credible, she would need to demonstrate *knowledge*—such as an understanding of the motivations of for-profit businesses and familiarity with the competitive position and business models of insurance companies. And she would do this work most effectively by making the appropriate impression on the people she engaged with on the job, which is to say by displaying certain *traits*—in this case a polished, businesslike manner of interaction with colleagues, partners, and other leaders.

Why does this matter? Competencies, and their underlying behaviors, are generally not specific enough to help one think through how to help future leaders develop or acquire what they will need to succeed. One has to get to the level of skills, knowledge, and traits to think through development plans for individuals or hiring needs where gaps can't be filled.

## GuideStar: Reevaluating Needs after a Change in Course

GuideStar faced an inflection point when it changed its funding model to one based primarily on fees for services. Changing the model meant changing the culture, as well, toward a more market-driven culture of a for-profit business. GuideStar realized that it needed a team that was committed to the mission but also had skills and experience in meeting the needs of customers. "It wasn't a question of either-or, for-profit or nonprofit," said Debra Snider, GuideStar's vice president for operations. "We needed both. [But] that [still] meant attitudes had to change."

To help bring about that change, GuideStar brought in marketing and sales professionals from private-sector businesses. Their job wasn't just to rethink GuideStar's revenue-generating operations. They also served as role models who taught by example the customer and market focus that would enable the organization to successfully execute its new, customer-centric operating model. The infusion of new competencies had its intended effect: By the end of 2011, earned income made up nearly 100 percent of GuideStar's revenue. Foundation funding supported only special projects and the development of new business lines.

GuideStar's transition prompted it to ask what new competencies its team needed to develop. In the sidebar "Questions to Ask When Assessing Future Leadership Needs," you'll find a list of questions that can help your senior leadership team start thinking about leadership talent, succession, and competency gaps.

Your organization may be embarking on a change in course that raises similar questions. How your organization answers those questions can profoundly influence its leadership development efforts. To increase your odds of successful execution it is important to answer the questions early on and in as much detail as possible. We have observed that when nonprofits fail to go deep enough when linking changes in strategy or business model to leadership, they struggle to define the specific activities and assignments that will instill the necessary attributes in their future leaders. Problems most commonly arise when nonprofits:

- fail to specify in sufficient detail how their business models will change and how that change will affect their activities and operations, including what their leaders must do differently to succeed, and

- focus on generic competencies, such as "the ability to work productively with others," rather than on the specific behaviors needed to successfully execute the organization's strategy. For example, a nonprofit organization that plans to enter into a commercial partnership to deliver a new program doesn't simply need leaders who can work productively with its partner. It needs leaders who understand what the partner hopes to gain from the relationship and who can frame a discussion of the program in terms of the value it can create for the partner. By going into this sort of depth when considering their leadership needs, organizations can provide developing leaders with the underlying skills and experiences that would enable the behaviors that the strategy requires.

Two nonprofits, Endeavor and CARE USA, illustrate the value of a considered, detailed approach to reassessing leadership development in light of a business-model change. Both organizations have embarked on collaborations, which many nonprofit leaders and social sector experts have told us will be critical to the future effectiveness of nonprofits. Their experiences illustrate a crucial point about collaborations: They come in a wide variety of shapes and sizes. One form of collaboration is to ally with another nonprofit to deliver a program. Another is to join or lead a coalition of multiple stakeholders. Partnering with a government agency or for-profit company is yet another type of collaboration. Merging with another nonprofit is still another. And each type of collaboration requires different leadership behaviors for success.

Endeavor and CARE USA are pursuing collaborations that on the surface appear similar. Both organizations are forging partnerships with local organizations. But those partnerships are built on very different business models. The result is that their leadership requirements differ accordingly.

## Two Different Collaborations, Two Different Sets of Leadership Needs

Endeavor, which selects and mentors high-impact entrepreneurs from around the world to help grow their businesses, has collaborated with Abraaj Capital, a leading private equity firm in the Arab Gulf region, since 2010. The experience has enabled Endeavor to specify that its future leaders need to understand the needs and marketing strategies of this partner.

On the other hand, CARE, a leading humanitarian organization that fights global poverty, has learned through its work with local nongovernmental organizations that its future leaders will need the ability to build local partners' capacities to carry out their joint projects. That means leaders need the ability to transfer CARE's knowledge and management skills to its local partners.

How can organizations reach this level of specificity *before* they implement a new model? We believe that by thinking ahead in a systematic fashion, they can ensure a snug fit between strategy and future leadership needs and development.

**Tying Leadership Development to Strategy: A How-to**

To facilitate the work of thinking ahead, we recommend that nonprofits engage in a process that we have developed and used with several clients. It helps them prepare for a significant change in strategy or business model and craft a leadership development plan to address the change. The process is guided by the answers an organization gives to four sets of questions:

- **What major strategic change(s) or business model change** are we making?

- **What do we need to do well** to successfully execute these strategic changes?

- **What behaviors will our leaders need to do these things well? What skills, knowledge, and traits drive those behaviors?** (For more on the distinctions among behaviors (and competencies), skills, knowledge, and traits, see the sidebar, "Leadership Development Terms Defined.")

- **Which specific leadership needs link to specific leadership positions?** Can we develop the required behaviors in our own staff in time to fill those positions as they open up? If we cannot, what is our plan for recruiting outsiders who demonstrate these behaviors?

## Questions to Ask When Assessing Future Leadership Needs

- What will be the organization's strategic priorities during the next three to five years?

- What organizational capabilities will be required to achieve those priorities?

- Which leadership roles directly link to solving, executing, or implementing actions necessary to achieve those priorities?

- What skills are critical for these roles? How do these differ from those required today?

## Step 2: Assess the Potential of Your Staff (Current and Future Leaders) to Take On Greater Responsibility

Once your current leaders have mapped out your organization's future leadership needs, they're ready to take a step back and candidly consider whether members of the staff have the potential to move into leadership roles. At larger organizations, this talent review might include current leaders and their direct reports one or two levels below them in the hierarchy. Smaller organizations can broaden the review to include the entire staff.

**Tool:** On the next page, you'll find a Sample Performance-Potential Matrix used in many for-profit and some nonprofit organizations to structure conversations about employee potential and development needs.

# Sample Performance-Potential Matrix

| POTENTIAL | | | |
|---|---|---|---|
| **High** | May be new to role; ensure support is available<br><br>May be in wrong role; consider reassignment | Continue to develop in current role; consider providing test assignment in more senior role | Consider providing significant new assignments or reassign to a more senior role |
| **Growth** | May be in the wrong role or at the wrong level; consider providing test assignment in different role | Continue to develop in current role | Gradually expand current role |
| **Limited** | Consider replacing if support has not improved performance | Continue to develop in current role; periodically reassess potential for growth | Retain in current role; periodically reassess potential for growth |
| | **Below expectations** | **Meets expectations** | **Exceeds expectations** |
| | | **PERFORMANCE** | |

Source: Kemp & Watson, Omidyar Network

The matrix draws on both past performance and senior leadership's judgment about an employee's potential to take on greater leadership responsibility, plotting both evaluations on a two-dimensional graph. It then highlights potential next steps related to growth and development. Obviously, this assessment isn't an exact science. But it is possible for you and your team to make an informed judgment about staff trajectories that takes into account your organization's unique culture and style of working, as well as its future leadership needs. We can offer some general guidance on using this tool to extract valuable information about your staff's potential.

To plot performance along the horizontal axis, determine whether an employee is performing below, at, or above expectations in his or her current role. That means that your organization needs to have in place clear criteria regarding performance expectations and a regular practice of performance assessment. This will allow you to place the employee in the appropriate column along the axis.

Then consider whether the employee is likely to succeed in a more significant role. Again, doing this well requires clear, agreed-upon criteria. These criteria, like those measuring current performance, will vary from one organization to the next. But it's helpful to consider more than sheer ability. We recommend that you also take into account the employee's career aspirations and level of engagement in your organization's mission and activities. (For more on how to assess potential, see the sidebar "What 'Leadership Potential' Really Means," which adapts the Corporate Leadership Council's suggested definition of potential to a nonprofit setting.) In other words, an individual's placement along the vertical axis isn't simply a question of whether he or she could take on a greater leadership role. Consider whether the individual wants a greater role and is likely to remain with your organization. That judgment will determine in which row you'll place the employee along the vertical axis.

# What "Leadership Potential" Really Means

The term "leadership potential," at first glance, can seem too subjective to be useful. But the Corporate Leadership Council has developed a detailed model of high potential that we have modified for use in the nonprofit sector. (Our main modification was to deemphasize the motivating power of purely financial rewards.) This model can help organizations identify the most promising internal candidates to fill their leadership pipelines. High potential, according to the Corporate Leadership Council, has three components: **aspiration**, **ability**, and **engagement**. The individuals who score high on all three dimensions are your organization's high-potential leadership candidates.

**Aspiration** is a term that captures the intensity of an individual's desire for:

- Results and recognition
- Advancement and influence
- Intrinsic (and, to a lesser extent, financial) rewards
- Work-life balance
- Overall job enjoyment

Employees with a strong desire for things like results, recognition, advancement, and influence—and willingness to make necessary trade-offs in other areas to get them—have the high aspirations that mark high-potential leadership candidates.

**Ability.** Of course, there's more to leadership potential than aspiration alone. High-potential individuals also display strong ability; that is, the combination of innate characteristics and learned skills needed to carry out their day-to-day work.

- Innate characteristics include cognitive abilities and emotional intelligence; and
- Learned skills including technical, functional, and interpersonal skills acquired through classroom or on-the-job learning.

**Engagement** completes the high-potential triad. It consists of four elements:

- Emotional commitment: The extent to which employees value, believe in, and enjoy the organization where they work
- Rational commitment: The extent to which employees believe that staying with the organization is in their best interest
- Discretionary effort: The willingness of employees to "go the extra mile" for the organization
- Intent to stay: An employee's willingness to remain with the organization

Employees who score high on one or two dimensions of leadership potential can be valuable contributors to your organization. But it's the **employees who can put together the total package—aspiration, ability, and engagement**—who have the highest potential to rise to your organization's key leadership roles and succeed in them.

**The Development Dialogue at Year Up**

Year Up, which works with urban young adults to help them reach their full potential through professional careers and higher education, uses its own version of a performance-potential matrix to review its staff members. Year Up's senior leadership team has been reviewing staff potential since its earliest days, when the team would meet in founder Gerald Chertavian's living room to discuss each staffer's development needs.

Now that the organization has grown, things are a bit more formal. Senior leaders meet annually with line managers to consider staff members' potential, with three purposes in mind. The first is to **help managers think more systematically about their teams' strengths and development needs and then to hold managers accountable for the progress of their team members**. Are a manager's direct reports moving up and to the right on the matrix over time? The answer helps senior leaders evaluate the manager's abilities as a talent developer. The meetings also **give managers, especially newcomers to the role, an opportunity to discuss staff development issues with their peers.**

The meeting's third purpose is to **help senior leaders create detailed development road maps for their direct reports and the organization**. This information supplements data gathered in performance reviews and in the regular development conversations that managers have with their direct reports. Year Up uses each person's location on the performance-potential matrix as a starting point for thinking about whether the person is in the right role and how to help the person move forward. Basic questions emerge: How can his or her manager (and other leaders) help the person grow and improve in the job? Is the employee ready for a new role or for a stretch assignment that will help him or her prepare for a role with greater responsibility?

Managers come to the meeting with initial assessments of their staff members, but those assessments aren't the last word. Other managers have a chance to offer input and correct any bias that might creep into the assessments. Many managers have an understandable tendency to rate all their team members above average. Input from other managers and comparison against other departments' staff help leaders form a more rounded assessment and zero in on specific development needs. "Once the group gets talking, they eventually arrive at a common understanding," said Year Up Chief Operating Officer Sue Meehan. "It's a process of dynamic revision."

It's worth reiterating that a successful evaluation of leadership potential involves more than assessing a staff member's job performance and abilities. Managers and other leaders also need to gauge each employee's career aspirations and engagement, which contribute just as much to leadership potential as sheer ability. By being systematic about considering these often overlooked factors, organizations can get an accurate reading of their staff members' leadership potential. Organizations have various ways of gathering information about aspirations and engagement. GuideStar employees, for example, meet quarterly with their managers to discuss not just their current job performance but also their growth and development. Youth Villages, which provides services to emotionally troubled youth and their families, asks new hires whether they're interested in relocating or finding other career options within the Youth Villages network. The organization uses this information to identify staff to consider for positions at new sites and to assess its ability to staff new sites with existing employees. While there are many additional steps required to set up a new site, this process gives the Youth Villages expansion team a head start on assessing its future needs.

As helpful as these conversations can be to employees, they may be even more helpful to senior leaders, who can factor what they've learned from leadership potential assessments into their development planning. Sometimes they learn from the assessment process that internal development alone will not be enough to meet the organization's leadership needs.

# Step 3: Create Your Plan A for What Leadership Teams within the Organization Will Look Like in Three Years

Given your future needs and your current staff, are you likely to have the leaders you need when you need them? Can you meet your needs through internal development or will you need to hire from outside the organization as well? One way to answer those questions is to prepare a Plan A, which can be described as a first draft of the future. As noted, we borrowed the concept and terminology from American Express Corp., where CEO Ken Chenault regularly asks senior leaders to develop leadership road maps for their departments or divisions. As the name suggests, Plan A doesn't attempt to be definitive—after all, every Plan A presupposes the need for a Plan B. But it represents senior leadership's best estimate of how the organization and its leadership needs are likely to change in the medium term, and it's subject to revision as new information becomes available.

Our advice is to create a Plan A that projects out three years, pulling together the information gathered in Steps 1 and 2. Again, these are to 1) define the critical leadership capacities needed to fulfill your organization's mission in the future and 2) assess the potential of your staff (current and future leaders) to take on greater responsibility. Ideally, your work in these steps will give you enough information to envision the team you will need and identify the people who are ready to step into leadership roles immediately as well as others who could be prepared to assume leadership roles in a few years' time, provided they develop certain competencies or meet specific development goals. These people might be referred to as "leadership candidates," and your Plan A is developed from that pool, as well as from external hires. In the following sidebar you'll see two exhibits, one listing a hypothetical organization's leadership candidates for various roles and the other the Plan A developed, in part, from that list. Your leadership candidates list and Plan A may look something like this, though the specifics will change, depending on your organization's structure, strategy, and staff.

Of course, there's no guarantee that your Plan A will come to fruition. Elements of the plan will probably change with time, as candidates' aspirations change, new roles are added, or leaders unexpectedly depart. As a result, the plan will need periodic revisions—a morph to Plan B. But the revision process itself can be valuable, by revealing weak or nonexistent pipelines for certain roles, highlighting critical developmental needs, and clarifying what roles will have to be filled through external hires.

We wish to reiterate here a point we made in the introduction: The Plan A discipline is different in crucial respects from typical succession planning. Most succession planning discussions tend to focus on the present or near term, and they generally aim to maintain the status quo by filling existing roles with people whose competencies replicate, as closely as possible, those of current incumbents.

Plan A, by contrast, is future-oriented: It's a vision of how the organization's goals, activities, and strategy are likely to change over time, and how leadership competencies and roles will have to change to keep pace. Many aspects of the organization might not change at all. But if, for example, its business model evolves as GuideStar's did or if it expands its roster of services, the organization may need to create new roles or fill existing roles with leaders possessing different competencies. In such cases, a typical succession plan won't meet the organization's needs. Plan A, with its focus on the future, prompts leaders to think about how to develop or hire the people best-suited to lead a changed organization. When hockey star Wayne Gretzky was learning the game as a boy, his father, Walter, often told

him, "Skate where the puck's going, not where it's been." [8]
Plan A helps organizations skate where the puck is going.

# Sample List of Leadership Candidates and Plan A

The following two exhibits express the vision of a hypothetical CEO for her senior leadership team in three years. The organization is growing rapidly and will need greater management capacity to achieve its goals. Five people currently report to the CEO, and she expects to add a CFO to the team within a year. She also anticipates that her chief development officer (CDO) will retire soon. Through the performance-potential conversations she has conducted, she has learned that her CDO believes that the manager in charge of individual giving is willing and able to take on greater responsibility. But the CDO also believes that the organization's emerging funding model will require this candidate to develop her skills with corporate and foundation donors, and implement a development metrics dashboard. The internal candidates for CFO, on the other hand, need several years of seasoning before they'll be ready to step up. Therefore, the organization will have to recruit a CFO from outside. There's one other key position up for grabs: This CEO does not have a COO. But one of her program directors has the potential to take on greater organization-wide operational responsibilities. If he does so successfully, he may be promoted to senior program director. (Note that this plan addresses an organization's senior-level leadership pipeline. But it's also adaptable to other levels of the organization and may be useful to department heads as well as CEOs.)

---

8 McKenzie, Bob (1999). "Walter's World." In Dryden, Steve. *Total Gretzky: The Magic, The Legend, The Numbers.* McClelland & Stewart Inc., Toronto.

# Sample leadership candidates list

| Key Role & Current Leader | Leadership Candidates | Year Ready (est.) |
|---|---|---|
| Jane Michaels **Executive Director** | 1) George Mendoza **Program Director** | 2017 |
| | 2) Sarah Miller **Program Director** | TBD |
| Sarah Miller **Program Director** | 1) Jack Underwood **Program Manager** | 2014 |
| George Mendoza **Program Director** | 1) Bianca Cruz **Sr. Program Manager** | 2014 |
| | 2) Chris Herold **Program Manager** | 2016 |
| TBH 2014 **Sr. Program Director** | 1) George Mendoza | 2015 |
| Tom Smith **Chief Development Officer** | 1) Cynthia Reed **Manager of Individual Giving** | 2014 |
| | 2) Sue Evans **Manager of Corporate Philanthropy** | 2015 |
| Ellen David **HR Director** | 1) Melody Jackson **HR Manager** | 2016 |
| TBH 2013 **Chief Financial Officer** | 1) Frank Vasquez **Sr. Finance Analyst** | 2016 |
| | 2) Bethany Harrison **Finance Analyst** | TBD |

# Sample Plan A

| Key Role | 2013 | 2014 | 2015 | Comment |
|---|---|---|---|---|
| **Executive Director** | Jane Michaels | Jane Michaels | Jane Michaels | No change. |
| **Sr. Program Director** | n/a | n/a | George Mendoza | George should take on additional operational roles across 2013-14; if he delivers, he will move into this Sr. Program Director role in 2015, continuing to oversee the program area as well as add further organizational responsibilities to his portfolio. |
| **Program Director** | George Mendoza | George Mendoza | n/a | If George is promoted, this role will be replaced by the new Sr. Program Director role in 2015. |
| **Program Director** | Sarah Miller | Sarah Miller | Sarah Miller | No change. |
| **Chief Development Officer** | Tom Smith | Cynthia Reed | Cynthia Reed | Cynthia should use 2013 to build her skills with corporate and foundation donors, and implement a development metrics dashboard; if she delivers, she will be ready to move into the CDO role. |
| **HR Director** | Ellen David | Ellen David | Ellen David | No change. |
| **Chief Financial Officer** | TBH in 2013 | TBH in 2013 | TBH in 2013 | TBD – This will likely be an external hire, due to the junior finance bench. |

Source: Adapted from American Express Corp. template

## Why You Need a Communications Strategy

Organizations undertaking leadership assessment and planning for the first time will want to think carefully about how to talk about the process within the organization. Should potential candidates be notified that they're being considered for future leadership roles? What information should be shared with employees who are not considered high-potential? What information should be shared with the organization as a whole, and what should be held in confidence by senior leadership, managers, and individual employees? Without recommending any particular course of action, we strongly suggest that senior leaders develop a communications strategy that takes into consideration the culture of their organization before they embark upon the leadership assessment process, beginning with a clear statement of the goals of the planning process.

Questions to be posed include: What is the organization hoping to achieve? To reach those goals, who must be engaged and how? What will people want to know about the process, and where are they likely to direct their questions? Given the sensitivity of these issues, it's important for senior leaders to understand the answers to these questions thoroughly before they engage in related conversations with employees. Organizations where such conversations are culturally ingrained have a head start when formulating their communications strategy.

# Get the Ball Rolling: Understanding Your Future Needs

**Tips for those at an early stage...**

**Gather your senior team** for a once-a-year offsite meeting to discuss the organization's future; use this input to create a Plan A for the senior team:

- Start with a discussion of where the organization is going and what the likely leadership needs will be in three years or so.

- Use the performance-potential matrix described in this chapter to assess the team's direct reports.

- Use the information from this discussion, together with your one-on-one conversations with senior team members, to create a Plan A for the senior team.

- Update your Plan A annually and share it with the board.

**...and at a more advanced stage**

**Ask senior team members to create Plan As** for their departments:

- Think about how the department's mandate is likely to evolve over time and the new capabilities that will be needed.

- Assess the potential of staff to grow into those roles using criteria such as each individual's ability, engagement, and aspirations.

- Include the preparation of these plans in senior team members' annual goals and hold them accountable for creating them.

## How the Nature Conservancy Talks about Development

The Nature Conservancy (TNC), a global organization dedicated to protecting and conserving ecologically important lands and waters, has a carefully crafted communications strategy for its development conversations. It asks leaders in each of its regions to identify succession candidates among its employees—people with "the ability, aspiration, and engagement to rise to, and succeed in, more senior, critical positions." Nothing is secret about this process: Employees across the organization are aware of the ongoing selection process and of the criteria for selection.

The organization makes sure that every employee knows that all employees are entitled to professional development, whether it takes the form of leadership development or of training in functional skills. Succession candidacy, in other words, is just one of several pathways to professional growth. And succession candidates are made aware that their candidacy isn't a permanent designation—it can change over time, depending on the candidate's aspirations, performance, and engagement, as well as the organization's overall goals.

Conversations between managers and their reports play a crucial role in the selection and development process. Managers of potential succession candidates conduct formal conversations aimed at gauging the employee's aspirations and willingness to relocate, take on new assignments, and acquire new competencies. For example, TNC believes that these qualities spell the difference between employees with high ability and those with high potential—that is, between those who are strong performers in their current roles and those who have the potential to take on more responsibility. Individuals selected as succession candidates receive special support and opportunities, such as new assignments and participation in TNC's global training programs, but they also face heightened expectations. They know their advancement depends on their continued high performance and willingness to take on stretch assignments and relocate, if necessary.

TNC believes it's just as important to communicate with people not selected as succession candidates. Managers talk to these employees to address any concerns about their future with the organization and to map out alternative development plans and career opportunities. TNC wants its employees to understand that succession candidacy isn't the only way to grow within the organization.

TNC's communications strategy incorporates some of the best leadership development practices identified by the Corporate Leadership Council. For example, TNC emphasizes frequent conversations that don't just discuss current job performance but also encompass career potential and career aspirations. These conversations, the Corporate Leadership Council has found, are an effective way to deepen employees' engagement in their own development and reinforce the sense that they have a meaningful future with the organization.

These conversations also help TNC's leaders keep pace with the changing goals and aspirations of the organization's employees. Employee aspirations, after all, are neither uniform nor static. Not everyone wants to be a CEO or is willing to relocate. Some people may even want to slow down due to changes in their private lives. Others may need time to mature and settle into their current roles before setting their sights on advancement. The conversations are also a necessary reminder to employees that candidacy for a leadership position guarantees nothing—advancement is contingent on continued high performance and development.

To be sure, these conversations can be difficult—it isn't easy for an employee to hear that his or her performance does not meet expectations or that he or she appears to lack the ability to advance in the organization. And it isn't easy for managers to deliver bad news. Many managers will need guidance and coaching to keep such conversations constructive and handle the emotions they can stir up. But as difficult as these conversations can be, they're also necessary. By regularly checking in with employees on their performance and development, managers can avoid unpleasant surprises and address potential roadblocks to advancement while there is still time to address them.

## Building a Diverse Team to Address Future Needs

Many nonprofits are attempting to build greater cultural and demographic diversity in their senior ranks—not just because it's the right thing to do, but because they believe diversity at the top is critical to their ability to serve diverse constituents and to empower diverse communities. In the words of one senior leader, "Our movement is rooted in issues of class and race...our leaders have to be diverse to sort this out."

How nonprofits define diversity varies depending on their mission and context. Those focused on social justice within the United States, for example, are often seeking to develop a more racially and ethnically diverse set of leaders, including those from disadvantaged communities. Global NGOs are more likely to wrestle with questions of expatriate versus in-country representation. Both groups may find that they have fewer women at senior levels or in certain types of roles than they would like.

When executed well, all the processes discussed in this guide can contribute to building a diverse leadership team, but the process of understanding future needs, described in this chapter, is key to getting it right. Each step can help your organization go about building a diverse team with a clearly defined strategic intent.

- When you engage in the first step of this process, "defining the critical leadership capabilities required for the future," you can make a detailed statement of your diversity needs, laying out what capabilities are needed to succeed, in what roles, and in what time frame.

- When assessing potential in the second step, you have an opportunity to identify where you are on track, where you need to step up development efforts to prepare diverse internal candidates for future leadership roles, and what gaps need to be filled externally.

- In the third step, developing Plan A, a vision is set for having the right leaders in key roles.

From one step to the next, your organization will be able to develop, refine, and update its diversity plan.

As you build a diverse team of leaders, the processes described in other chapters will be relevant as well. In 2011, the National Human Services Assembly (NHSA) commissioned a study to identify practices increasing ethnic and racial diversity of senior management within Assembly member organizations. The study's findings underscore the value of succession planning. In the NHSA's words, "organizations that bring diversity into succession planning give themselves an opportunity to course correct and bring talent into their leadership pipeline." The study also recommended several actions that closely echo the steps discussed in this guide:

- CEOs and boards who make a business case for diversity
- Performance measurement systems that establish clear goals
- Mentoring to support diverse talent
- Accountability systems that hold senior leaders accountable for results

We are not implying that developing a diverse senior team is no different than building any other set of competencies in the organization. All over the world, we see that barriers to equity are deeply entrenched and slow to fall, and the process of increasing diversity will likely be more complex than any effort to build new functional skills or add new positions to the organization. But for nonprofits that have identified diverse leadership as mission-critical, the processes in this guide should serve as a strong foundation for progress.

For more on the topic of diverse talent in the nonprofit sector and a complete list of the NHSA's recommendations, see the NHSA's "Developing Senior Management Diversity" and Commongood Careers & Level Playing Field Institute's "The Voice of Nonprofit Talent: Perceptions of Diversity in the Workplace."

# The Rest of the Story

*You've had long days before, but this was a doozy. As you reflect in your office after the meeting, you take stock of all you and your team have accomplished. You have mapped out the next three years for your organization and come to a pretty fair estimate of your changing leadership needs. The members of your team came prepared with a Plan A for their departments, assessing their staffs' potential to fill the leadership gaps you've identified. You were surprised at how much discussion the assessments generated and how widely the assessments of some individuals differed, at least at first. But it was actually kind of inspiring to see people arrive at a consensus once they had talked through their concerns. And you know that the team will get better at these conversations over time and with practice.*

*To cap off all your efforts, you were able to begin revising each team member's Plan A, and have gained an overall view of the changes ahead for the organization and the leadership competencies you'll need to bring those changes about. Now all you have to do is work with your people to develop those competencies. That's the next big discussion.*

# Chapter 3: Developing Your Future Leaders

*It's late, and the rest of the staff has gone home. Well, that's only fair—you're the CEO, after all. In the quiet of your office you reflect on the activity of the past several months. You've done the groundwork. You have committed yourself, the board has signed on, and the message has gone out to the entire organization: Leadership development is a strategic imperative. You have put in long hours with your colleagues assessing the organization's present and future leadership needs, and together you have identified the people with the potential to fill crucial leadership roles in the years ahead and their development needs.*

*Great. You pause for a moment to congratulate yourself, and then take a deep breath.*

*You know you've only just begun.*

*Now it's time to get to work developing your potential leaders, equipping them with skills and capacities they need to be effective leaders today and even more so tomorrow. You know it won't be easy, but you also know it's vital to the long-term health of your organization. And you have the 70-20-10 learning model to help you organize your efforts. Recognizing that leadership development occurs largely on the job, you and your team are ready to map out a set of work assignments that will challenge your high-potential staffers to acquire new competencies, skills, and capacities. That's 70 percent of the battle. Will this learning model work as advertised? You're about to find out.*

In this chapter, we look at the four-step process for developing leadership at any nonprofit. It's up to you to decide how to bring these steps to life at your organization. That will change depending on the organization's size, structure, and style of working, not to mention the specifics of its Plan A. The steps themselves are what's important. They provide a guide to creating an organization where leadership development is all in a day's work.

In fact, if there's one thing we hope you'll take away from this chapter, it's that leadership is learned by doing. That's why many corporations—and a growing number of nonprofits—use the 70-20-10 model as their blueprint for leadership training. As its name suggests, the model calls for 70 percent on-the-job training, supplemented with 20 percent coaching and mentoring, and 10 percent formal training. It's an effective way to fulfill your Plan A vision for your future leadership team. You'll find a more detailed discussion of this in the sidebar "The 70-20-10 Model."

## The 70-20-10 Model

Business concepts go in and out of fashion with bewildering speed. But one concept that has stood the test of time is the 70-20-10 leadership development model. Pioneered by the Center for Creative Leadership and based on 30 years of study of how executives learn to lead,[9] it rests on the belief that leadership is learned through doing. There's plenty of evidence to support that belief, including a study by the Corporate Leadership Council that concluded that on-the-job learning has three times more impact on employee performance than formal training.[10]

---

9 See for example "Grooming Top Leaders: Cultural Perspectives from China, India, Singapore, and the United States," September 2011. www.ccl.org.

10 The Corporate Leadership Council Human Resources. www.clc.executiveboard.com.

As the 70-20-10 name implies, the learning model calls for 70 percent of development to consist of on-the-job learning, supported by 20 percent coaching and mentoring, and 10 percent classroom training. The model has spread widely in the corporate and nonprofit world, with various organizations putting their own imprint on it.

The 70-20-10 model's three components reinforce one another, adding up to a whole that's greater than the sum of its parts. The model builds on research showing that human beings retain information most effectively when they gain it in a practical context. Learning is even more powerful when the lessons of experience are reinforced through informal discussion with people who have performed similar work. These veterans can point out common pitfalls, offer practical advice, and help steer the learner away from bad habits.

To emphasize the value of experience, however, is not to slight the importance of formal learning. But formal learning is most valuable when it supplies technical skills, theories, and explanations that apply directly to what is learned through experience—and when it is both valued and quickly integrated within the work environment. In studying their own leadership development programs, for example, American Express found that the effect of formal training increased significantly when the participants' manager engaged with them on the training both before and after the training session.[11] Training was most effective when:

- The learner had one-on-one meetings with his or her immediate manager to discuss how to apply the training in his or her specific role.

11 American Express Corp., "The Real ROI of Leadership Development: Comparing Classroom vs. Online vs. Blended Delivery."

- The learner perceived his or her manager endorsed and supported this specific training.
- The learner expected to be recognized or rewarded for the training-related behavior change.

The lesson for nonprofits is clear: Leadership development programs are only as good as the managers who encourage their direct reports to apply what they have learned.

The good news is that many nonprofits are offering their employees challenging on-the-job assignments. A majority—69 percent—of respondents to Bridgespan's Leadership Development Diagnostic Survey agreed or strongly agreed that their organizations "have sufficient quality opportunities for employees to gain new leadership skills via on-the-job opportunities." But it's not clear that those opportunities are designed with the clear intent to build specific competencies, as a Plan A would call for. Only 35 percent of respondents agreed or strongly agreed that "employees with the potential to move into leadership roles have development plans in place that identify areas for development and sources of development support." And follow-up is lacking. Only 46 percent of respondents agreed or strongly agreed that "employees are held accountable for and evaluated on their progress on their development plans."

The survey results suggest that many nonprofits could benefit from a more systematic approach to leadership development, with plans tied to existing HR and performance management processes. In this chapter, we'll outline steps you can follow to weave leadership development into your organization's activities. It's a collective effort that involves the CEO and other senior leaders, line managers, and employees themselves, who play an active part in crafting their individual development plans.

## Four Steps to Developing Future Leaders the 70-20-10 Way

- Step 1: Cultivate talent champions.
- Step 2: Identify organizational needs and craft development opportunities.
- Step 3: Co-create individualized development plans.
- Step 4: Follow through on development plans.

### Are You Effectively Developing Future Leaders? An Excerpt from Our Leadership Development Diagnostic Survey

Are the following statements true of your organization?

- Your performance management processes (e.g., annual evaluations, goal setting) support effective leadership development and succession planning.
- Employees with the potential to move into leadership roles have development plans in place that identify areas for development and sources of development support.
- Employees are held accountable to and evaluated on their progress on their development plans.
- You have sufficient quality opportunities for employees to gain new leadership skills via on-the-job opportunities (e.g., stretch assignments, new projects in their existing roles).
- You have sufficient quality opportunities for employees to gain new leadership skills via mentoring and coaching.

- You have sufficient quality opportunities for employees to gain new leadership skills via formal trainings.

- The development opportunities you offer to employees are effective in building more capable leaders.

- Employees view your organization as a place where they can develop their leadership skills.

- Employees are supported through their transition when they move into a leadership role.

# Step 1: Cultivate Talent Champions

As the 70-20-10 model implies, line managers are the key players in the leadership development process. They do the heavy lifting by working with high-potential leadership candidates every day and overseeing the vast majority of their development through on-the-job learning and individual coaching and mentoring. So the first task of senior leaders is to develop line managers into what the Corporate Leadership Council refers to as "talent champions"—managers who recognize the vital importance of developing a cadre of up-and-coming leaders and take responsibility for preparing them. Effective talent champions make a measurable impact on their organizations: The Corporate Leadership Council has found that in the corporate world, talent champions outperform their peers in meeting business goals, delivering 7 percent higher business unit revenue and 6 percent higher business unit profits than average.[12] And it's reasonable to think that talent champions can help nonprofits perform better, too.

But the Corporate Leadership Council also has found that only 19 percent of managers in the corporate world might be

---

12 Corporate Leadership Council Human Resources, *Corporate Leadership Council Talent Management Effectiveness Survey*, CEB.

# The presence (or lack) of talent champions

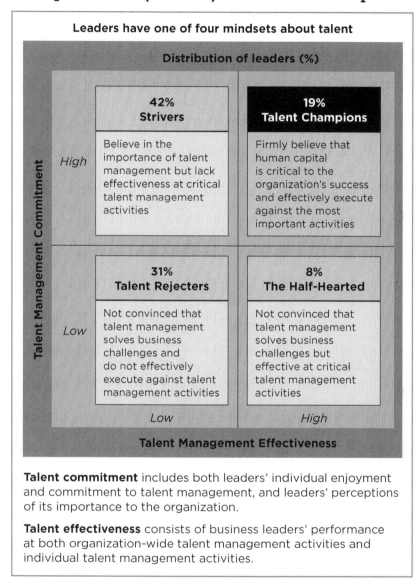

**Leaders have one of four mindsets about talent**

**Distribution of leaders (%)**

|  | | Low | High |
|---|---|---|---|
| **Talent Management Commitment** | **High** | **42%**<br>**Strivers**<br><br>Believe in the importance of talent management but lack effectiveness at critical talent management activities | **19%**<br>**Talent Champions**<br><br>Firmly believe that human capital is critical to the organization's success and effectively execute against the most important activities |
|  | **Low** | **31%**<br>**Talent Rejecters**<br><br>Not convinced that talent management solves business challenges and do not effectively execute against talent management activities | **8%**<br>**The Half-Hearted**<br><br>Not convinced that talent management solves business challenges but effective at critical talent management activities |

**Talent Management Effectiveness**

**Talent commitment** includes both leaders' individual enjoyment and commitment to talent management, and leaders' perceptions of its importance to the organization.

**Talent effectiveness** consists of business leaders' performance at both organization-wide talent management activities and individual talent management activities.

Source: Corporate Leadership Council Human Resources, *Corporate Leadership Council Talent Management Effectiveness Survey*, CEB.

characterized as "talent champions." The good news is the Council's finding that an additional 42 percent are "strivers," eager to take on the work of developing others but lacking the skills needed to do it effectively. Assuming a similar segmentation exists among nonprofit managers (indeed, we expect the percentage of strivers may be higher in nonprofits), organizations can make significant progress by cultivating the would-be talent champions in their managerial ranks.

And indeed, talent champions can be developed. In the first two chapters we highlighted several high-impact actions that the CEO and senior leaders can take to promote leadership development. They can:

- Make the case for investing in leaders with a clear vision of the link between leadership development and achieving impact.

- Integrate leadership development processes into existing work processes, such as monthly or quarterly check-ins, senior team or department meetings, and annual reviews.

- Hold senior leaders, HR, and others accountable for leadership development by setting goals and reviewing progress against Plan A, and stepping in when a senior leader's actions run counter to the leadership development norm.

- Reinforce all of the above by investing in developing the senior team—and asking the board to make the same investment in the CEO.

These are crucial activities because they model leadership development behaviors for the rest of the organization. In addition, by singling out talent champions for recognition, the CEO and senior leaders can highlight examples of high performance, where a leader is successfully developing others. This type of soft accountability or peer pressure can be even more powerful than formal job requirements, particularly when coupled with coaching and training in areas where managers are struggling.

Support is especially important when working with first-time managers or managers just making the transition from managing individuals to managing groups. These managers often lack all the skills to fulfill their role as talent champions, coaches, and mentors. Their work experience may not have prepared them to think of themselves as talent developers. They may also need help changing their work habits and time allocations to make room for these unfamiliar responsibilities. Focusing support and development efforts on individuals transitioning into managerial work can pay big dividends, as first-timers acquire leadership development skills—and the leadership development mindset—as they learn the other skills needed for their new jobs.

That approach is rewarding KIPP, the charter-school management organization that provides high-quality education to some of America's neediest children. Recognizing they were stretched thin by rapid growth, KIPP's leaders made a considered decision to make the organization's school principals and grade-level and subject-matter leaders—in effect, their line managers—champions of the leadership development process. They reinforced this message by revising their leadership-competency model to put greater emphasis on people management. And to make sure school leaders were equipped to manage and develop talent, they convened gatherings where school leaders could meet with peers to discuss their challenges, share the leadership development methods that worked, and coach one another in talent and leadership development. The organization also created opportunities for up-and-coming managers to shadow school leaders. As they followed these leaders, the up-and-comers gained practical insights into being a talent champion, insights they were able to put into practice when they transitioned into leadership roles.

Recognizing the difficulties young teachers faced when jumping to a leadership role, KIPP created support materials designed to ease the transition (see the exhibit on the next page "Support for Leadership Transitions at KIPP"). The materials explained the competencies that new principals and other school leaders needed to cultivate and advised them on structuring their time for maximum effectiveness. Perhaps most important, the support materials helped new leaders with the shifts in perspective and time that their new roles required—for example, from focusing on a single class's academic performance and behavior to attaining school-wide results, or from focusing on developing their students' abilities to developing the abilities of their fellow teachers. By emphasizing talent development from the outset, KIPP is sowing the seeds of a leadership culture.

# Support for Leadership Transitions at KIPP

(Excerpts from the KIPP Leader Progression Road Map: Grade Level Chair to Assistant Principal)

## Competency shifts: Which competencies change the most?

| | |
|---|---|
| **Critical Thinking & Problem Solving** | • There are more challenges to anticipate and address, they are more complex, and impact the entire school.<br>• In addressing larger-scale/school-wide problems, you must consider a greater number of stakeholders.<br>• You must analyze, weigh options, and propose solutions more quickly than before. |
| **Decision making** | • You make decisions with an increased sense of urgency, and do so on a daily basis.<br>• You must publicly stand by difficult and controversial decisions that you (or the Principal) make.<br>• You are obligated to communicate decisions to many more stakeholders in a timely manner. |
| **Communication** | • You now frequently communicate to the entire school community.<br>• You must adapt your communication style appropriately across several different audiences within the school.<br>• You will periodically speak on behalf of the Principal. |
| **Impact & influence** | • You now often work through other school leaders (e.g., GLCs) to motivate and inspire students.<br>• You adapt your leadership style appropriately to influence diverse audiences in the school.<br>• You must be consistently persuasive in inspiring others to act. |
| **Performance management** | • You now work directly with teachers to set their individual performance goals.<br>• You now hold both teachers and grade-level teams accountable for results that roll up to the school level.<br>• You participate in managing formalized performance evaluation. |

Source: KIPP Leadership Progression Road Map, Grade Level Chair to Assistant Principal

# Perspective shifts: The changes in what you value and where you focus

| | | |
|---|---|---|
| Focusing on academics and behavior within the grade level | ➡ | Focusing on school-wide results |
| Focus on gaining the respect and trust of students and teachers in your grade level for leadership credibility | ➡ | Focus on gaining the respect and trust of all students and staff in the school for leadership credibility |
| Valuing GLCs who will provide helpful peer feedback | ➡ | Valuing GLCs who will carry the leadership team's message forward |
| Valuing your network of peers within your school for support and empathy | ➡ | Valuing networking with peers nationally across KIPP for support, empathy, and sharing best practices |
| Focusing on maintaining a presence among students in your grade | ➡ | Focusing on having a visible presence in most/all school-wide activities |

Source: KIPP Leadership Progression Road Map, Grade Level Chair to Assistant Principal

# Time shifts: The changes in your daily work

| | |
|---|---|
| Your core responsibility is instructional excellence within the grade | Your responsibility may be school-wide administration, discipline, or academics |
| Driving the grade-level agenda | Driving the school-wide mission |
| Mostly predictable daily tasks | Tasks that vary daily and may change unexpectedly |
| Building relationships with a limited group of students and teachers | Building relationships with all students and teachers in the school |
| Leading and coordinating a team of teachers | Leading and coordinating a team of managers |
| Providing coaching and informal feedback to teachers | Supporting formal performance management of teachers |
| Creating and managing instructional plans | Empowering GLCs to manage instructional plans |
| The majority of your work day is spent teaching in the classroom | The majority of your work day is spent outside the classroom |

Source: KIPP Leadership Progression Road Map, Grade Level Chair to Assistant Principal

# Step 2: Identify Organizational Needs and Craft Development Opportunities

The work of identifying the competencies that future leaders need flows naturally from the planning process discussed in Chapter 2, where you envisioned the organization's leadership needs in three years and mapped out a plan—Plan A—to develop or hire the people capable of meeting those needs. By the time you have prepared your Plan A and conducted the talent review, you will have a pretty clear idea of your organization's competency gaps. You and your leadership team can then study the organizational calendar and pinpoint the special projects, cross-cutting initiatives, board presentations, and the like where future leaders can gain experience. It's also a good time to zero in on any formal training or mentoring that, when coupled with appropriate on-the-job activities, might address the most glaring gaps.

If you have the time and the resources, you can also perform a more in-depth study of leadership competencies and the means of developing them. That's what Y-USA did recently, conducting a two-year study to identify the competencies its staff needed in order to meet the leadership challenges of the future and to provide a road map for developing them. Based on its findings, Y-USA created a comprehensive development guide, *Developing Cause-Driven Leaders*,[13] that identifies 18 competencies, grouped into four categories, and offers practical suggestions for developing them.

The Y's guide is a resource for any nonprofit committed to leadership development. But your organization can launch and sustain a leadership development program without going to the same lengths. The key is to identify ongoing activities

---

13 *Developing Cause-Driven Leaders: Leadership Competency Development Guide*, www.ymcachicago.org/page/-/pdfs/metro/Leadership%20 Development%20Guide.pdf.

that leadership candidates can engage in to develop needed competencies. Your organization offers plenty of opportunities to execute your Plan A by putting your rising stars in leadership situations, at little cost and with minimal disruption to operations. You could assign a leadership candidate to make an important presentation to your board or to important stakeholders, for example, or place several candidates on a cross-functional task force. Whatever the assignment, the Corporate Leadership Council recommends[14] that for maximum effectiveness, the opportunities involve four elements:

- **Discomfort**—Assignments should take candidates out of their comfort zones and call on skills other than those they have mastered.

- **Accountability**—Candidates must take ownership of their assignment and be held responsible for the results of their work.

- **Clarity**—The lesson the assignment is intended to teach should be clear to the candidate.

- **Relevance**—Each assignment should teach a skill or competency that leadership candidates need in their current roles, as well as in roles they may be asked to play in the future.

At the Y, leadership candidates who need competence in philanthropy, for example, are encouraged to research and write a grant proposal. The Y suggests that supervisors link the leadership candidate with an experienced grant writer who can explain the research process and furnish examples of successful proposals, and also give the candidate a suggested reading list. But it's the candidate's responsibility to prepare the proposal— an exercise well outside his or her comfort zone—and take responsibility for its results. The purpose of the assignment is clear, and its relevance to the candidate's work is plain.

---

14 "Unlocking the Value of On-the-Job Learning," www.ldr.executiveboard.com.

# Step 3: Co-create Individualized Development Plans

When senior leadership has identified the activities where future leaders can build their competencies, it's time for line managers to work with staff members one-on-one to create a development plan. These discussions can be built into the performance-evaluation process, which is a natural setting for discussing the skills that staff members need to do their current jobs effectively. It's not necessary, though, to prepare the individual development plan during the review meeting. Indeed, some organizations prefer to separate development and evaluation conversations to allow sufficient time and reflection for both conversations.

Whenever you schedule the development conversation, it's important to candidly discuss the staff member's aspirations, career trajectory, and goals. If a staffer wants a greater leadership role, there needs to be an honest assessment of the skills he or she must cultivate to get there. The staffer might need to work on several areas of performance, but as a practical matter, it's important to settle on two or three priorities. These are the areas to focus on during the coming review cycle.

When managers and a staffer have agreed on the development focus, they can turn to creating a development plan to address these needs. In our discussions with nonprofits, we have heard over and over again that the most effective plans reflect a true collaboration. Staffers who participate actively in crafting a development plan feel a sense of ownership they can't get from one they have inherited. It's up to managers to provide the support and guidance that staffers need to meet their development goals, but ultimately, it's the staffers' responsibility to carry out their plans and be accountable for its results. It's a responsibility that most people will be happy to take on if they feel like full partners in the planning process.

On the next page you'll see a simple template that Y-USA has created to help managers and staffers formulate development plans and fit them within the 70-20-10 framework. The timing for creating an individual's plan is left to each affiliate, but the national organization recommends beginning the planning process only after the formal evaluation is completed. This is to allow time to reflect and create a well-thought-out plan. Both the performance review and the staffer's self-assessment of leadership competencies (which staffers can fill out using an online Y tool) factor into the plan, which isn't complete until it includes training and coaching components, as well as on-the-job learning.

# Y sample development plan

**NAME:** Jill Sample | **LEADERSHIP LEVEL IN CURRENT ROLE:** Team Leader

**ASSESS DEVELOPMENT OPPORTUNITIES USING 70/20/10 LEARNING FORMULA*:**
Refer to the Leadership Competency Development Guide for suggested experience-based learning assignments, key coaching questions, formal training, self-study & valuable tips.

| I. Leadership Competency to Develop | II. Experience-based Assignments (70%) | Target Dates | III. Who will you ask to help? (and how?) (20%) | Target Dates | IV. Formal Training & Self-Study (10%) | Target Dates |
|---|---|---|---|---|---|---|
| **(a) Philanthropy**<br><br>(b) Behavior Description(s):<br>• Designs and conducts training programs for volunteers, staff, and other groups in order to educate them about the charitable nature of the Y.<br>• Secures gifts from prospective donors in order to generate financial support for the Y's mission. | 1. Give a presentation about the Y's mission impact and community benefit to a group of prospective members or donors.<br><br>2. Research opportunities and write a successful grant proposal. | By: 3/31/2011<br><br><br><br>By: 6/15/2011 | Sarah Brown, Chief Development Officer at my YMCA (possible coach or shadow opportunity)<br><br>Doug Robinson, Grant Writer for local school (could teach me to effectively conduct research and provide samples of grants)<br><br>Debbie Wagner, Senior Administrative Assistant (may offer tutorial for creating effective PowerPoint presentations) | Contact by: 1/20/2011<br><br>Set meeting: 2/28/2011<br><br>Contact by: 1/20/2011 | Read the book *How to Ask Anyone for Any Amount for Any Purpose* by L. Fredricks.<br><br>Attend AFP International Conference on Fundraising. | By: 2/01/2011<br><br><br>Scheduled: 3/20-3/23, 2011 |

**Select Leadership Certification:** ___ Working toward achieving a new Leadership Certification
___ Maintaining current Leadership Certification with 20 Leadership Certification Credits every 5 yrs & Assessment

**Circle Leadership Certification you're working toward achieving or maintaining:** Team Leader • Multi-Team/Branch Leader • Organizational Leader

*70/20/10 Learning Formula describes how leadership competencies are developed. 70% of learning and development comes from real-life, on-the-job experiences; 20% of learning and development comes from coaching, feedback, and from observing and working with role models; 10% of learning and development comes from formal training.

Source: Developing Cause-Driven Leadership®, Leadership Competency Development Guide, YMCA of the USA

# Get the Ball Rolling: Developing Your Future Leaders

**Tips for those at an early stage...**

**Meet twice a year** with each of your direct reports:

- Discuss their progress against their leadership development goals and work with each of them to identify the competencies they need to develop to grow as leaders.

- Reach agreement on the activities they can engage in to build those competencies considering the 70-20-10 framework discussed in this chapter.

- Allocate projects or initiatives so that staffers are doing work that develops the specific leadership skills they require and at the same time accomplishing the organization's objectives.

**...and at a more advanced stage**

**Build the number of talent champions** in your organization, particularly those striving to become more effective:

- Ensure your senior team is modeling effective development by creating and following up on development plans for their direct reports.

- Consider pairing strivers with proven talent champions who can help them raise their game.

- Consider developing guides for the management role—similar to KIPP's, described in this chapter—designed to make your managers more effective.

# Step 4: Follow Through on Development Plans

The best-laid plans have little impact if they sit on the shelf. That's why senior leadership must track the implementation of development plans and share their findings with the managers and staffers responsible for them. In organizations where development is ingrained in the culture, it's often enough for senior leaders to monitor progress informally, checking in with the people responsible and offering ad-hoc feedback and guidance. But organizations that are new to leadership development may want to institute formal tracking programs.

It's a good idea to schedule formal progress reviews at least semi-annually, and possibly more frequently in some types of organizations. Y-USA, for example, encourages managers to check in with staffers every quarter to review plan progress and make any adjustments. The check-ins usually don't take long, but they help ensure that there are no surprises during annual performance evaluations, when managers review each staffer's progress in meeting development goals. Project-based nonprofits might want to schedule reviews to coincide with major milestones in the project cycle. And it may be necessary to check in frequently with individuals who are struggling to fulfill their plans or who have just taken on significant new leadership responsibilities. To minimize disruption, these progress reviews should be tied into the organization's existing management processes and review cycles. The more closely they integrate into the workflow, the easier they'll be to implement and track.

## The Rest of the Story

*Whew. You have to admit (if only to yourself) that it was a little scary when you first considered the skills you'd need to develop in your leadership candidates to meet your organization's future needs. And it's true, some of your line managers are still finding their sea legs as talent champions. It's not easy for them to conduct the honest development conversations that your leadership candidates need to advance. That's why you have repeatedly touched on the topic during management team meetings. Good thing your COO is a born talent champion. The work she has done with her team is a real inspiration to your other senior team members. She has worked with her people to craft thoughtful individual development plans, and they have shown real imagination in choosing activities to build their leadership competencies. Now, of course, you'll have to keep a close eye on people to make sure they're putting their plans into practice. But that's all in a day's work—kind of like leadership development, come to think of it.*

*But (and there's always a "but," isn't there?) it's clear that you won't be able to fill all your organization's leadership needs internally. Your bench is a bit thin in a couple of places, and you're going to have to hire externally to fill some critical positions. There are some good candidates out there, but your organization has its own way of doing business. How can you be sure the people you hire will fit in and start contributing to your Plan A on Day One? OK, that's your next challenge.*

# Chapter 4: Hiring Externally to Fill Gaps

*Late-night phone calls are part of the CEO's job, but you never expected to hear from one of your longest-serving, most reliable senior leaders. He did yeoman's work as a member of the search committee that found the new site manager who starts tomorrow, but now he's having last-minute worries. He wonders if the organization will welcome your new hire. Will she adapt to the culture and the new leadership role? Can she work well with the other members of the site management team and form strong relationships with the board, community leaders, and the people the organization serves? Can she drive the change the organization needs to better fulfill its mission? With so many unanswered questions hovering about, his concern is understandable.*

*You reassure him as best you can. You remind him you didn't rush into this hire. You took the time to verify that the skills your organization needs simply couldn't be found in-house. You've conducted a patient search, one that engaged key voices inside and outside the organization. And you've thought hard about ensuring a smooth transition. Have you done enough? Tomorrow, you'll begin to find out.*

One chapter in a guidebook won't dispel all the uncertainty of the hiring and on-boarding process. But if you have carefully studied your organization's leadership needs and concluded that no one in your development pipeline has the potential to develop the skills needed in a key role, we can offer some practical advice that can help you and your organization hire the right person, help him or her make the transition into the new job, and start fulfilling your Plan A on Day One. Our advice grows from our past executive search work with more than 200 nonprofits. It has taught us a great deal about what goes into a great hire—and what can go wrong. One big lesson is that there are concrete steps you can take to markedly improve the likelihood that your new hire will be everything you hoped for, and then some. Of course, we can't cover the entire topic of hiring. Instead, we have focused on several essential processes that many nonprofits overlook or underplay. (For more resources on hiring externally, see the sidebar "More Help with External Hiring.")

## More Help with External Hiring

To learn more about the external hiring and integration process, you can consult our library of resources on the topic, which can be found at www.bridgespan.org. These resources include:

- "A Guide to Engaging an Executive Search Firm"
- "Writing the Job Description"
- "Conducting Successful Interviews"
- "Extending an Offer"
- "Making the Right Hire: Assessing a Candidate's Fit with Your Organization"
- "The Reference Check: More Than a Formality"
- "Managing a New Employee's Transition"

As discussed in Chapter 2, "Understanding Future Needs," you may discover after drawing up a Plan A for your organization or department that you cannot fill a critical leadership position internally. It may be that your organization is adding new sites at a rapid clip and doesn't have enough internal candidates to fill the site director vacancies. Perhaps your CFO has unexpectedly retired or taken a job with another organization, leaving behind a finance department whose senior employee is a financial analyst with only two years' experience. Or maybe you are planning a new initiative that calls for skills that the organization simply hasn't needed before.

Whatever the reason, you need to hire externally. Judging from our Leadership Development Diagnostic Survey, most nonprofit leaders feel reasonably confident that they're up to the task. Over three-quarters (79 percent) agree or strongly agree that they "effectively screen external leadership candidates to ensure they are correct for the role and the organization." And 79 percent agree or strongly agree that external candidates seeking leadership roles are attracted to their organizations.

Yet respondents are less sure of their ability to help new hires navigate the transition into their jobs. Thirty-eight percent disagreed or strongly disagreed that their organizations "on-board and successfully integrate external leadership hires." In our experience, successful on-boarding calls for thoughtful action throughout the hiring process. Well before the search begins, organizations that on-board successfully have reached clear internal agreement about what the organization needs in a given role. They rigorously vet job candidates and engage in on-boarding practices that build the new hire's capability and credibility. With those requirements in mind, we focus in this chapter on three key steps:

- Step 1: Define requirements for the role.

- Step 2: Create opportunities for both the organization and the candidate to assess whether the candidate is a good fit.

- Step 3: Design an on-boarding process that supports the new hire's capabilities and relationship development.

## Are You Hiring and On-boarding Outside Leaders Effectively? An Excerpt from Our Leadership Development Diagnostic Survey

Are the following statements true of your organization?

- You hire from external sources primarily when the capabilities required for a position are difficult to develop internally.

- External candidates seeking leadership roles are attracted to your organization.

- You effectively screen external leadership candidates to ensure they are correct for the role and organization.

- You on-board and successfully integrate external leadership hires.

Now let's walk through each step.

# Step 1: Define Requirements for the Role

Success in external leadership hiring begins with a clear statement of the requirements for the role the organization is trying to fill—one that everyone involved in the hiring process buys into. Without a shared understanding of what your organization needs to fill a given role successfully, you will have a hard time sourcing high-quality candidates and selecting promising candidates for further consideration.

Obviously, a clear definition of the organization's needs and requirements is crucial when you're hiring to fill a newly created role, but it's just as important when hiring externally to fill a vacancy. Hiring a replacement or successor gives your organization an opportunity to reassess the role and determine whether its requirements have changed as your organization's strategy has evolved or the leadership team has changed. It's also an opportunity to ask whether the experience of past incumbents in the role has exposed any gaps in the job description. You may already have performed this reassessment when you examined your organization's future needs as part of the process outlined in Chapter 2.

To create a clear, detailed definition of what the role and your organization require, you'll want to refer to your Plan A, where you have specified the competencies a given position will require. You also need input and leadership from the right people in the organization, whether or not you also hire an external search firm. We strongly recommend that a senior leader act as hiring manager. There's nothing wrong with tapping the expertise of your HR department or a search firm, but the role of hiring manager is too important for the senior leader to delegate. When seeking a new senior leader, it's also helpful to form a search committee to focus on the search from start to finish. Members of the committee should be willing and able to devote several hours to committee activities each week. Committee members who participate only sporadically will lack the background information and credibility needed to make the right final decision.

We have found that the most effective search committees are relatively small. A well-chosen group of three to four allows for a diversity of perspectives and expertise without burdening people or becoming unwieldy. But as the process unfolds, you will probably want to seek the input of other people in the organization. Peers, direct reports, and people who interact frequently with the role can offer their views on its most crucial functions, and what it requires in terms of seniority and tenure. It's often a good idea to bring these internal stakeholders into the process when the role is being defined and again during final-round interviews, when their evaluations can help spell the difference between a successful hire and a misfire. At these critical junctures, you might also want to include people who are currently successful in the role you're trying to fill, as these people are keenly aware what it takes to do the job well. If your organization does not have multiple people in the same role, you can instead invite the participation of someone who filled the role successfully in the past.

### The Search Committee Defines the Nonnegotiable Requirements of the Position

Your list of job requirements will be rooted in the skills the leaders of your organization will need as it evolves, based on the Plan A you created in Chapter 2. At the outset, the list may well be rather lengthy, as committee members construct an image of the ideal leader. But it's important to realize that the image is just that—an ideal—and that it's often not possible to find one person who embodies everything the committee is looking for. It may be necessary to make trade-offs in the course of whittling down the list to the five or six critical attributes that a person must possess just to be considered a plausible candidate.

This whittling-down process can engender intense, even heated debate. But it's important to bring to the surface any differences of opinion before the committee arrives at a final list of a half-dozen or so nonnegotiable requirements. Unless committee members fully air and resolve their differences and agree on what really matters in the role, the organization risks hiring someone based on ambiguous or conflicting job requirements. Not even the best-qualified new hire can meet expectations that aren't clearly stated.

### Two Approaches to Defining Role Requirements

Year Up, the nonprofit that works with urban young adults, takes a methodical approach to its external hiring. It always seeks leaders from the community when it sets up new sites.

When gearing up to hire an ED to succeed the founding ED of the New York site, it formed a search committee composed of representatives from the national office as well as from the New York site. They collaborated on defining the role's core responsibilities and describing the ideal candidate's traits. Their initial discussion revealed some sharp differences of opinion about the role's core responsibilities and requirements: Should the ED focus on new initiatives and programs, for example, or concentrate on providing stability and continuity? In the end, the committee needed about an hour of questioning and debate to come to a consensus about the role's requirements. And they revised that list after meeting several candidates and assessing how their description of the role matched up with the available talent.

KIPP, one of the nation's largest operators of charter schools, takes a somewhat different approach. When searching externally for new leaders, it uses its leadership competency model to assess the strengths and weaknesses of its existing leadership team and draws on its findings to shape its search for candidates. KIPP has learned from experience hiring regional COOs that the role can differ significantly from one region to another. In some regions the COO's primary role is to reduce the ED's internal workload, freeing up the ED to pursue external initiatives. In other cases, the COO is hired to complement or strengthen the ED's skill set, while in others the COO is being groomed for the ED role.

## Take Culture into Consideration When Hiring

Cultural considerations play a large role in determining the nonnegotiable requirements for the role you want to fill. We have found in our executive search work that many organizations are more rigorous and systematic when defining functional skill and competency requirements than when describing their culture. Yet a shared understanding of the organization's culture and of the personal attributes that ensure a good fit will help your organization make consistent hiring decisions, even when different groups of people are involved.

Many of the most successful nonprofits emphasize culture in their external hiring. Year Up, for example, makes it clear to hiring managers and job candidates alike that the organization is fast-growing and fast-paced. Its culture requires people who are comfortable with rapid change, have a high tolerance for ambiguity, and are ready to pitch in without being asked. Those attributes weigh as heavily in hiring decisions as functional skills.

But without a shared understanding of culture and cultural requirements, hiring managers can easily default to hiring people who simply remind them of themselves. As a result, they may bypass more suitable candidates and in some cases impair the organization's ability to create a diverse team.

How does an organization arrive at a shared understanding? Some larger organizations with established HR infrastructures have codified statements of values or cultural norms, and those statements are embedded in their leadership competency models. Many other organizations, though, have not considered the question of culture in a systematic way. It's important to do so before hiring a senior leader. At the very least, the search committee will want to think about the organization's work environment and the norms that govern interactions between people in the organization. Which behaviors does it reward, and which behaviors will it not tolerate? Candidates whose style of working and personal interaction clashes with those norms and expectations will be a poor fit, no matter how well they might perform the job's functional requirements. In the sidebar "Determining a Candidate's Cultural Fit," you'll find a series of questions that can help you define your organization's culture and determine whether a candidate is likely to fit within it.

# Determining a Candidate's Cultural Fit

**Will a job candidate feel at home in your organization's culture? What will the candidate bring to the organization's culture? Here are some questions to reflect upon in the course of your search.**

Before deciding whether a candidate belongs in your organization's culture, you need to have a clear idea of what that culture is. There are many ways to assess your organization's current culture, ranging from conducting an extensive organizational assessment and audit to simply sitting down and thinking through what types of people have succeeded at your organization. At a bare minimum, asking the following questions about your current organizational culture can help clarify what type of work environment your organization offers to potential candidates.

**Work Style**

- How do we get our work done? Collaboratively? Independently? A combination?

- How do we make decisions? Consensus-driven? Authoritatively?

- How do we communicate? Verbally or in written form? Directly or indirectly?

- What are our meetings like? Serious? Lighthearted? Tightly or loosely structured?

**Professional Opportunities and Advancement**

- What types of people tend to do well here? Individual contributors? Team players? People who are proactive or more responsive?

- How are we structured? Hierarchical or flat? Centralized or decentralized authority? Clear reporting structures or matrix?
- How do we reward people who do well?
- What happens when people don't perform well?

**Work Hours and Commitment to Work**

- How many hours a week do we expect senior management to work on average?
- Do we provide flexible work schedules or allow for telecommuting, or do we prefer people to work set hours?
- How much travel do we expect of senior management?
- Are we looking for someone who will be here for a certain number of years or as part of a succession plan for senior management?

**Architecture, Aesthetics, and Atmosphere**

- How are our offices set up? Open environment? Closed-door offices?
- How do we dress? More formally? Less formally?
- How do we have fun?

When you have arrived at a working definition of your culture, consider what you are looking for in a senior manager beyond the job description. Though your goal may be to find a candidate who fits well within your organization's culture, that does not necessarily mean you should look for someone who is a cookie-cutter image of the rest of your management team. It is critical to balance your search for fit with your goal of building a team with a diverse set of backgrounds, experiences, ideas, and working styles.

- What kinds of senior management personalities and work styles exist in our organization?

- What adjectives would we use to describe the people who have been successful in our organization?

- What kind of decision-making style do we want this new senior leader to have? Are we looking for an approach that is similar to the ED's or for a different, complementary style?

- Are we looking for someone to create more teamwork within the organization or to establish more authority and hierarchy?

- What kind of leadership style are we looking for in this position? Someone who will promote what has worked so far or someone who will shake things up within the organization?

- Are we looking for a senior leader with more "gravitas" or someone who will lighten up the existing team?

- What types of personalities work well with the various stakeholders we interact with and what characteristics will this person need to have in order to be successful in these interactions?

*Adapted from "Making the Right Hire: Assessing a Candidate's Fit with Your Organization," accessible at www.bridgespan.org.*

# Step 2: Create Opportunities for Both the Organization and the Candidate to Assess Whether the Candidate Is a Good Fit

Once you have hammered out your list of job requirements, you're ready to identify a slate of candidates with the potential to meet your organization's needs. It's tempting at this point to proceed as quickly as possible. Our advice: Don't rush. It takes time to find the right person, and a hasty hire can ultimately cost your organization more in terms of money and momentum than a thorough search would. Build enough time into your search process to allow you and your candidate to get to know each other. Remember, you're not looking to make a quick sale—you're building a relationship.

Ideally, your search calendar will give candidates adequate time to familiarize themselves with your organization's culture and leadership team. They'll have a chance to get a sense of how their role might evolve over time. They might discover that their scope of responsibilities and the role's priorities are likely to evolve in a direction that's incompatible with their aspirations. Better to learn that before they're hired than after.

When Year Up was searching for an ED for its New York office, it was careful to give candidates plenty of opportunities to familiarize themselves with the organization and the role they'd be asked to fill. Going into the process, Year Up's search committee agreed that candidates needed to meet the people they'd be working with if they were hired and learn the specifics of the Year Up culture and the nature of the ED role. The committee mapped out a series of activities that enabled each candidate to do just that. The slate of activities varied according to the candidates. A candidate with extensive private-sector experience but little recent experience with students, for example, was given several opportunities to interact with students. This gave Year Up's search committee a chance to evaluate the candidate's aptitude for what is a major part of the ED's job and the candidate a chance to learn whether he enjoyed the work. Candidates also met EDs at other Year Up sites, and interacted frequently with the people who would be their direct reports in the New York office and with other staffers at the site.

The information gathered flowed in two directions. Candidates gained a detailed understanding of Year Up's culture, people, and activities. The people of Year Up, meanwhile, had a chance to size up the candidates and form a judgment about their suitability for the ED job. By building these "get acquainted" opportunities into its process, the search committee deepened its knowledge of each candidate and enabled it to make a hiring decision based on far more information than that found in résumés and references.

One of the most important lessons we've learned from the nonprofits we've worked with is that successful searches go beyond the standard interview questions and give decision makers a chance to learn about how a candidate might actually operate. They create opportunities to see how candidates make decisions and interact with colleagues. It's not really feasible to learn in detail about every candidate's operating style, but once your search committee has winnowed the roster to two or three candidates, you start to probe more deeply. One approach asks each finalist to study detailed information about the organization, such as its strategic plan, operating statements, and records of board deliberations. Then the committee can ask each finalist questions like:

- If you got the job, what would be your priorities in your first 90 days? In your first year?

- After a year on the job, how would you know if you were on the right track? How would you measure your progress?

- Given what you know about our organization, what is your vision of where we could be in five years?

Your organization's leaders will have answers to these questions, and you can't expect that your candidates' answers will match. After all, your leaders know the organization far better. But the candidates' answers are a good indicator of their understanding of the organization's mission and culture and can give your committee a sense of their strategic focus and overall fit. The answers also help assess each candidate's knowledge of the resources and capabilities of your organization and the challenges and opportunities it faces. They also weed out candidates who offer only superficial, boilerplate replies or whose vision for the organization diverges sharply from leadership's.

Inviting a candidate to join in a working session with the senior leadership team is another good way to measure potential. By participating in a real meeting to solve actual problems, the candidate gets a chance to contribute to the group's work. How does the candidate influence the group dynamic? Does he or she add to the group's energy or drain it? Does the candidate improve the team's performance or disrupt it? The answers to these questions will help the committee decide whether the candidate is right for the role.

In addition to assessing what the candidate has to offer the organization, communicate what the organization has to offer to the right candidate. This discussion is much more than a sales pitch. It's also a good way to help both the candidate and your organization decide whether a relationship benefits both sides—ideally for a long time to come. Financial compensation and the opportunity to advance the organization's mission will be a part of this discussion, of course, but only a part. Many other factors can influence a candidate's decision, such as the opportunity to work with other senior leaders to develop a particular skill or expertise, exercise autonomy in an entrepreneurial role, or advance long-term career plans. Some candidates might welcome the opportunity to associate themselves with a well-regarded organizational brand or work in a particular kind of culture.

# Step 3: Design an On-boarding Process That Supports the New Hire's Capabilities and Relationship Development

Some of your most important work begins *after* a candidate accepts your offer. Even the most promising career can be short-circuited if the on-boarding process goes awry. That's why it's crucial to approach on-boarding thoughtfully and systematically, surrounding the new leader with support during the transition. And remember, on-boarding doesn't happen overnight, so be prepared to offer support for at least the first 30 to 90 days of your new senior leader's transition.

A successful on-boarding process has many moving parts, but our discussion will focus on three of the most important factors: managing the transition, establishing key priorities and goals, and forming key relationships that help integrate the new hire into the culture.

**Managing the Transition**

Even before your new hire arrives, you can begin passing along helpful information, such as minutes from your last management meeting. And you can arrange opportunities to meet key employees and board members. Invite your new hire to any special events to interact with staff members. Such interactions facilitate understanding of the organization's activities and concerns before Day One.

If circumstances permit, it's often helpful for your new hire's tenure to overlap with that of his or her predecessor. During this period, the predecessor can gradually hand over responsibilities and help the newcomer solidify relationships with key colleagues and become more familiar with the organizational culture. It's important, though, not to prolong the transition period. We have found that if the transition lasts longer than a month, people in the organization begin to suspect that the new hire is a slow learner or that the predecessor is reluctant to let go of the reins. By the end of the month, the new hire should be visibly in charge and the predecessor out the door, although that doesn't mean that all communication between them must cease.

### Establishing Priorities and Goals

It's important for the new hire to work with his or her supervisor early to establish three to five key goals. Supervisors can help them succeed by alerting them to potential obstacles and risks and by regularly checking in with them on progress. During the busy on-boarding period, when new hires are proverbially drinking from the fire hose, these check-ins help them set priorities and start making a visible contribution.

## Get the Ball Rolling: Hiring Externally to Fill Gaps

**Tips for those at an early stage...**

**Identify gaps in the leadership pipeline:**

- Using your assessment of future needs, identify the areas where you will likely need to hire externally and those where you should aim to fill positions internally.

- Think about the leadership competencies that external hires will need to succeed at their roles in the future.

**...and at a more advanced stage**

**Get a fix on your organization's culture** and the kind of people who thrive in that environment:

- Use the cultural questionnaire in this chapter to help guide your thinking.

> - Think about the kinds of activities that can help you assess whether a job candidate is a good cultural fit—an informal, get-acquainted dinner with you and your senior staff, or perhaps participation in a problem-solving session with the senior team.

## Forming Key Relationships

We have stressed that the on-boarding period is a crucial time in a new hire's career. It's the time when the new hire forms key relationships and is integrated into the organizational culture. Some of the best-regarded nonprofits facilitate this process by assigning advocates to help new hires find their bearings in the organization. The advocates' job titles are of secondary importance. What matters is that they understand the organization, know its strengths and weaknesses, and are familiar with the leadership team. Effective advocates are recognized throughout the organization as culture carriers and enjoy the affection and respect of staff and leadership.

Judy Vredenburgh credits a board member for her successful on-boarding as CEO of Big Brothers/Big Sisters of America (BBBSA). Joe Connolly, chairman of the BBBSA board and head of the search committee that recruited Vredenburgh, took her under his wing and served as her sounding board and advocate during her first months on the job. "He really acted as my coach and helped me transition successfully," Vredenburgh, who has moved on to head up Girls Inc., told us. "In part, it was his thorough understanding of the way the organization operated; in part, it was also his deep understanding of the organization's culture." Connolly, she says, helped her gauge how much change the organization could withstand and how quickly. They developed a solid relationship based on trust that enabled Connolly to raise issues that other staff members were reluctant to bring up. "I would have to say that the key was not his position as the board chair," Vredenburgh said, "but rather his personality and knowledge. What mattered is that he understood the organization, and he understood me, and I felt I could trust him."

Year Up takes a somewhat different approach to the advocate role, one that fits its networked organizational structure encompassing sites in nine US cities. When Year Up opens a new site, it recruits an ED from the local community and transfers one or two employees from elsewhere in the network to help get the site up and running. These employees do more than help set up the new facilities. They're explicitly recognized as culture carriers—a prestigious role at Year Up. Employees must apply to become culture carriers, and those chosen for the role enjoy a special status. They're recognized for their commitment to the Year Up mission, their excitement at helping the organization grow, and their willingness to pitch in wherever they're needed.

The culture carriers play several critical roles in the on-boarding process. During the early days of a site's existence, they're busy performing the responsibilities of their functional job title, which varies across culture carriers. (Past participants have included program instructors, admissions directors, and operations staff.) At the same time, they're introducing the new ED to people around the organization who can provide resources, advice, and organizational know-how "for those aspects of the job you only learn about when you're actually doing the job," in the words of COO Sue Meehan. For example, a culture carrier might connect the new ED to an ED who is familiar with the problem of students who miss classes because they're homeless. The culture carriers are also heavily involved in interactions with students, modeling for the new ED the organization's practice of finding teaching opportunities in everyday moments. The culture carrier might use an interaction with a student who's dressed inappropriately to talk about why it's important to dress properly for work. "They're really showing the new ED how to live Year Up's values," Meehan said. And in the end, living your organization's values might be the most important part of your new hire's job.

# The Rest of the Story

*Your senior team member is no longer worried. Indeed, he sheepishly admitted the other day that he can't quite remember why he was so worked up. Your new site manager has been on the job about two months, and it's almost as if she's always been there. Thanks to the time and energy you invested to define precisely what the organization needed from her, she had a clear idea going in just what she had on her plate. And because your search process included several opportunities for your new hire to meet her new colleagues, she greeted them like old friends when she arrived in the office. One of your most trusted colleagues has taken it upon himself to introduce her to people she can turn to with questions that pop up during the work day and point her to organizational resources she can tap for answers. Yes, you think to yourself, she's going to work out fine.*

*But how is the rest of your leadership development initiative working out? Are you seeing results? What aspects of the initiative are working better than others? And how can you improve the parts of the initiative that are less than satisfactory? That's our next and final discussion for making the most of your Plan A process.*

# Chapter 5: Monitoring and Improving Practices

*So far, so good. With you pointing the way, your organization has made critical decisions and initiated a suite of processes that can help ensure that your organization will have the leaders it needs today and in the future to meet its strategic goals. Now you face what may be your most difficult and important task: maintaining your leadership development effort's "cruising speed." You have to find ways to sustain your leadership development processes and keep up the intensity of the effort after the initial rush of enthusiasm. One reliable way to keep the momentum going is to continuously monitor your leadership development processes as you would any of your organization's other critical functions, to learn which processes work and which could stand some improvement. That's what management is, after all: confirming that you have set in motion the key processes called for in your plan— in this case, your Plan A—and measuring their effect on the organization. What you really want to learn is whether you have created organizational momentum for leadership development so that it becomes integrated into every team member's everyday activities.*

The nonprofit leaders we have surveyed admit that of the five processes discussed in this guide, the process of measurement and continuous improvement is their weakest link. Among the respondents to our Leadership Development Diagnostic Survey, only 3 percent strongly agree and 16 percent agree that they "have established clear goals to guide their leadership development efforts." And only 24 percent agree or strongly agree they "regularly collect data to evaluate [their] progress and to understand what leadership development practices and supports are most effective."

We'll therefore devote this chapter to some basic approaches organizations can take to start learning from their leadership development efforts in order to enhance their practice.

In our conversations with leaders and organizations struggling with monitoring, we often heard a strong desire to identify the "killer metric" that could definitively quantify a return on their leadership investments. While valuable, that type of analysis can be quite challenging and may not be the best place to start (see the sidebar on page 135 "Should You Compute Your Leadership Development ROI?"). The goal of monitoring, after all, is quite simple: to help you learn whether your efforts are producing the leaders you will need. Where the efforts are falling short, you want to find out why and fix what isn't working. Where efforts are going well, you want to shine a light on what's working and do more of the same. The key, we believe, is to begin with four steps, which we will detail in this chapter. They are:

- Step 1: Confirm objectives and key actions you're prioritizing.
- Step 2: Create checkpoints to ensure accountability.
- Step 3: Assess whether you're meeting your goals.
- Step 4: Diagnose potential problems and adjust course.

A well-designed monitoring system produces reliable information about your entire organization's leadership development performance. High-performing organizations get that way by stressing *individual* follow-through and accountability. So while we'll be focusing on organizational performance in this chapter, we will also elaborate on individual responsibilities, especially in the second step, where we discuss creating checkpoints to ensure accountability.

## Are You Monitoring Progress Effectively? An Excerpt from Our Leadership Development Diagnostic Survey

Are these statements true of your organization?

- You have established clear goals to guide your leadership development efforts.

- You regularly collect data about your leadership development practices to understand whether they are effective.

- You take action on the data you collect to improve leadership development practices.

- As changes to organizational strategy occur, you update your leadership development goals and practices accordingly.

## Step 1: Confirm Objectives and Key Actions You're Prioritizing

There's no doubt about it. Monitoring practices can be daunting, especially for something as multifaceted and difficult to quantify as leadership development. To knock the problem down to manageable size, begin by stating as clearly and comprehensively as possible what you are trying to achieve. The vision of the future and the development goals compiled in your Plan A can help organize your thinking. After all, the aim of leadership development, stated simply and broadly, is to ensure that your organization has the leaders it needs to achieve its goals and fulfill its mission, today and in the future. Your Plan A encapsulates your strategy for reaching your target, and you should be encouraged that you've already gone a long way toward ensuring that outcome by preparing a Plan A and following the steps laid out in this guide.

Now it's time to gauge the results of all that hard work to make sure that what you are doing is getting you there. First, it can be extremely helpful to summarize the decisions and commitments you've made regarding leadership development. You may have identified areas of relative weakness, as identified through our Leadership Development Diagnostic Survey tool at www.bridgespan.org/LeadershipDiagnostic. But most important is to summarize the specific actions and initiatives you're taking to build up the leadership pipeline as identified in your Plan A, discussed in Chapter 2. You can then determine whether those actions are having the desired effect (selecting those feedback measures is something we discuss more in Steps 3 and 4).

One way to organize your summary is to create a table like the one on the opposite page, where we've provided hypothetical examples of goals, actions, and feedback desired. The actual specifics will vary.

Now, with your priorities in front of you, you can turn to the information you'll need to measure how well your organization is performing the tasks it has set for itself. What you're looking for is information that will tell you:

- Whether you're complying with the action plan you've drawn up;
- How you're progressing against your leadership goals; and
- How effective your actions have been in meeting your leadership development goals and whether (and how) to adjust.

These are the guiding questions that each of the following steps will address.

# Sample leadership development priorities

| STRATEGIC PRIORITIES | DEVELOPMENT GOALS | REQUIRED ACTION | NECESSARY FEEDBACK |
|---|---|---|---|
| Q: What are the organization's strategic priorities? | Q: What are the desired outcomes for our leadership development efforts? | Q: What are the critical actions needed to accomplish these goals? | Q: What information do we need to gather & assess in order to know how we're doing? |
| • Double the number of youth served in current geographies by opening new sites. | • Develop 5 new site managers in the next 3 years. | • Provide cross-functional development to potential site leaders (e.g., budgeting, stakeholder engagement). | • Number of potential leaders ready now, in 6 months, 18 months <br> • Impact of development on candidate readiness |
| • Develop significant new revenue sources to support growth. | • Build senior leadership team capabilities and capacity to support fundraising. | • Recruit senior director of development. <br> • Evolve leadership competency model and role descriptions to include fundraising. <br> • Pair leadership team members with board mentors to help build fundraising skills. | • Successful integration of senior director <br> • Impact of development on team's capabilities |

Source: Adapted from Omidyar Network

# Step 2: Create Checkpoints to Ensure Accountability

While external events and contextual changes can certainly derail plans, in our experience, the most likely culprit is a simple lack of follow-through. For any plan to have a chance of success, it has to be implemented. As an organization, you need to create checkpoints to ensure there is compliance with the actions to which you've committed. That's what Carolyn Miles, the Save the Children CEO whom we met in Chapter 1, does during the first quarter of every year. That's when she reports to her board on Save the Children's leadership development and succession pipeline. It's a chance for her and the board to check the status of key leadership development initiatives and establish a theme for leadership development topics to be addressed in the coming year.

You might want to consider following Miles' example, baking these status checks into your organization's existing processes. At Save the Children, senior leadership meetings are a regular item on the organization's calendar, and at least one each year is devoted to a group discussion about succession and talent planning. While some of the meeting is given over to a discussion of organization-wide leadership development needs and priorities, team members know they'll be held accountable for leadership development in their areas of responsibility—an ongoing reminder that leadership development is an important part of their jobs.

Each direct report also meets individually with Miles to review his or her performance against leadership development goals and set new goals for the coming year. In a separate meeting, she discusses with each team manager his or her individual development plan. Every step along the way gives Miles an opportunity to reinforce the message that leadership development is critical to the organization—and to effective job performance. It's also a chance to reinforce that one's own development is something that each employee has to own and drive.

You may decide that your organization should review its progress against leadership development goals more or less often than Save the Children. Whatever the frequency, it's important to confirm that you're executing the leadership development plan you went to so much trouble to create. You can do this without significant disruption to your organization's activities by adding these reviews to the agenda of existing meetings and check-ins. In doing so, you're not just ensuring that you're executing your leadership plan. You're also holding people accountable for doing so, especially the CEO, the board, and line managers.

### Who's Responsible for What?

**The board:** As discussed in Chapter 1, an engaged board can make a vital contribution to an organization's success. If you buy that leaders are critical to any organization's success—and you do, or you wouldn't have read this far—then the board has a responsibility to inform itself about the organization's Plan A and hold the CEO and the rest of the senior team accountable for executing it. At the successful organizations we've studied, the board reviews the status of the leadership pipeline at least annually and regularly updates itself on the organization's key leadership initiatives.

**The CEO and senior team:** As we have repeatedly stressed, no leadership development plan can succeed without a strong commitment from the CEO and senior team members. In Chapter 2 we discussed the senior team's annual talent review meetings, where team members review leadership needs, assess staff potential, identify gaps, and discuss required actions to develop the organization's leaders, prior to preparing a master Plan A. These meetings are themselves a critical checkpoint, but like Save the Children's

Miles, you may want to meet more frequently with the team to track implementation and assess the progress of particular initiatives. If you have created working groups or task forces to, say, refine your competency model or hire a key person, they should check milestones frequently. (For more on implementing large-scale organizational plans, see Bridgespan's "Living into Your Strategic Plan" at www.bridgespan.org.)

**Line managers:** Senior leaders can also support leadership development by modeling effective practices for line managers, who, as discussed in Chapter 3, are vital to any leadership development effort. By checking in with them periodically, you're doing more than instilling an ethic of individual accountability, as important as that is. You're also creating the opportunity to reflect on progress against your goals and the lessons you've learned. You also can identify areas for improvement.

## Step 3: Assess Whether You're Meeting Your Goals

There is no one right way to monitor progress. But as a general rule, you'll probably want to institute some sort of review of the actions you're taking to build your leadership pipeline and gather feedback to assess results. Two organizations with well-established leadership development efforts, KIPP and Save the Children, take different approaches to this task. We'll start with KIPP, which is currently in an ambitious growth phase. It wants to double the number of schools in its network by 2015. To meet this goal, it will need a slew of new principals. So naturally, KIPP wants to keep a close eye on its pipeline of potential school principals and track the number of people completing the progressive training needed to prepare them for increased leadership responsibility. (At KIPP, leaders typically advance from grade-level chairs to assistant principals to principals, often with intermediate steps in between.)

In contrast, Save the Children is a large and mature organization and has chosen to focus on creating a deep bench of potential successors for a handful of key positions in each division. It uses this talent-tracking information, along with a summary of each division's key development themes, as the basis for senior team talent-planning meetings and annual updates to the board.

Both KIPP and Save the Children gather the data that enables them to understand the status of their leadership pipeline. Of course, the status of your pipeline may be changing slowly and it may take several years to fully understand whether you are achieving your leadership development goals. So how can an organization get an early read on whether it is making progress or not? One approach would be to revisit the Sample Performance-Potential Matrix introduced in Chapter 2. Annually looking at your up-and-coming leaders on this grid provides invaluable information about individuals, as well as the overall status of the pipeline. A review might show, for example, that while individuals in one department are developing the needed competencies, the pipeline as a whole isn't filling as quickly as you'd hoped. It may show that some parts of the organization are building a more diverse bench of future leaders than others. That information may reveal areas that require more focused investigation, which brings us to our final step of diagnosing problems and adjusting course.

# Get the Ball Rolling: Monitoring and Improving Practices

**Tips for those at an early stage…**

**Set targets** for executing each set of "Tips for those at an early stage" found in each chapter of this guide:

- Report on your organization's progress against those targets to your senior team and the board.

- During annual goal-setting discussions with the senior team and the board, determine leadership development priorities for the coming year.

**…and at a more advanced stage**

**Fine-tune your monitoring and measurement efforts:**

- Determine where your efforts are meeting with the least success and collect data to help you pinpoint the cause of the underperformance.

- Look for cases of "positive deviance"—aspects of the program that are meeting with better-than-expected success.

- Apply what you learn from your successes to underperforming elements of the program.

- Expand your measuring and monitoring every year to include more elements of your leadership development effort.

# Step 4: Diagnose Potential Problems and Adjust Course

Leadership development processes and practices can always be improved, but there are only 24 hours in the day, and you can't assess everything all at once. So where do you begin? The simple answer is to start with any trouble spots identified in the previous two steps. If there are pockets of noncompliance or particular leadership roles where you have trouble retaining and progressing individuals, as revealed by the review of your Performance-Potential Matrix, then these areas merit in-depth analysis. On the flip side, you can gain powerful information by studying pockets of "positive deviance" within your organization—groups or leaders with a strong record of developing talent and producing new leaders. Analyzing their practices and approaches can help you isolate what works. As helpful as quantitative measures can be, there's nothing like success stories and internal role models to generate organizational excitement about your leadership development efforts.

If you are in the early days of formulating your leadership development system and don't have enough information on performance over time to identify particular trouble or bright spots, you might focus on practices that are new to the organization or those that you believe are most important. For example, if you identified providing cross-functional development opportunities as key to developing future site leaders, you may want to start collecting feedback on these experiences and assess whether they are developing the desired competencies.

One axiom rules all such efforts: It is important to gather feedback through a variety of methods.

If appropriate, start with basic data on the process or area in question. For example, to assess a new training program, you might start with the numbers and types of individuals who started and completed the program. Questionnaires and surveys can also be helpful to understand perceptions and satisfaction with the process or aspect in question. They can test whether training was linked to a broader development plan, as called for in Chapter 3, and whether participants discussed the training with their managers before and after the session. Both participants and managers can weigh in on whether participants were able to apply what they learned and whether desired outcomes were achieved (such as changes in knowledge).

It's usually a good idea to allow sufficient time to elapse after training so that both participants and their managers can reflect on how participants' behavior has (or hasn't) changed. Qualitative methods such as interviews, focus groups, and document reviews also can be used to determine whether the outcomes resulted from the process in question, particularly in the absence of a comparison group, or to assess the drivers or root causes of performance or nonperformance.

More important than the information you collect is what you do with it. The checkpoints you established in Step 2 of this chapter, in addition to fostering accountability, also provide venues to discuss the performance of the leadership development system and how it can be improved. Whether you're talking to the CEO, the board, the senior team, or managers on the front line, you can use the following questions to help guide your discussion:

- What lessons have been learned over the past year?
- What are the strengths and weaknesses of the system?
- Does the leadership development system allow the organization to meet its goals?
- What adjustments do we need to make?

These discussions, as well as any evolution of strategic goals, might spur you to adjust the leadership development system.

Perhaps you'll determine that you need to develop additional competencies in your potential leaders or provide them with new learning experiences.

As your leadership development systems and strategic goals evolve, you will likewise want to consider adjustments to your monitoring efforts. For example, as your strategy changes, you might want to update the table where you list your strategic priorities and leadership goals. Or you might select different parts of your leadership development system for more focused investigation. Whatever changes you decide to make, remember that the objective isn't to generate more data but to perpetuate a cycle of continuous honing of your leadership development efforts.

## Should You Compute Your Leadership Development ROI?

As the leader of a nonprofit, you might ask yourself (or your board or funders may ask you) whether you should try to compute your leadership development effort's return on investment (ROI). That is, should you calculate the effort's financial payoff, expressed as a multiple of the amount of money spent on it? There are certainly benefits for undertaking this kind of assessment. If you can demonstrate, for example, that the payoff for a pilot effort was four times the amount invested in it, you have a powerful piece of evidence that can persuade a skeptical board or funder to back a wider plan. And as we described in Chapter 1, Boys and Girls Clubs of America (BGCA) used the data generated by its study of ROI (compiled with the assistance of McKinsey & Co.) to rally its affiliates to the cause of leadership development.

But a few words of caution are in order before you decide to embark on the laborious process of calculating your effort's ROI. Gathering the data necessary to reliably compute ROI is enormously expensive and time-consuming. Even large corporations with ample resources and large staffs of monitoring and evaluation professionals have a great deal of trouble determining the ROI of various internal efforts. You may decide that for all its unquestioned value, the time, money, and organizational energy devoted to determining leadership development's ROI can be better spent elsewhere.

Many of the nonprofit leaders we've spoken with recommend that, at the very least, you focus first on putting in place systems and processes for gathering basic data on your plan. Because most leadership development occurs on the job, a logical place to start is to gauge whether your organization is providing its leadership candidates with enough on-the-job learning opportunities and whether line managers are stepping up to their coaching and mentoring responsibilities. Over time, you may be able to expand your focus to gauge what effect leadership development is having on organizational outcomes. Ultimately, you may decide to tackle the job of calculating the ROI of your efforts. But as we heard time and again from nonprofit leaders, don't focus on ROI at the expense of monitoring more basic data. Even if you don't perform your own calculation, you can always cite the ROI data compiled by organizations like BGCA to build support for your own leadership development efforts.

# The Rest of the Story

*And here you are, at the end of your journey. The funny thing is, you know you're also at the beginning of another one. Launching your leadership development efforts was a huge undertaking. Now it's time to ensure it's producing optimal results by monitoring your progress and reflecting on what is working and what isn't. No sense kidding yourself: It's going to take time and effort to keep tabs on leadership development. But at least you've had the good sense to knock the task down to manageable size by limiting your focus to a few carefully selected areas that will help you judge whether your development efforts are achieving the desired results. And you have already made plans to share what you've learned with your board, senior leadership team, and line managers. Like you, they're accountable for the results, and you're looking forward to hearing their ideas. Truth be told, you're kind of excited at the prospect of fine-tuning your processes over time. This could be the start of something big.*

# Chapter 6: Getting Started and Moving Forward

As we reach the end of this guide, we hope we have convinced you of something we said in the introduction: "... [L]eadership development isn't mysterious, accidental, or something that can be postponed. It is, rather, a systematic process that nearly every nonprofit can implement." We also hope we have convinced you that leadership development processes are worth the time, effort, and energy needed to execute them. After all, the future of your organization may depend upon it. Judging from our research, many nonprofits recognize that leadership development is an organizational imperative and would welcome the opportunity to learn about the best leadership development practices found in the nonprofit and for-profit sectors. We hope this guide goes some way toward meeting that need.

The processes that we detail here are designed to integrate leadership development into your organization's ongoing work activities. At the heart of this guide is what we, with a nod to American Express Corp., call Plan A—a vision of your organization's future leadership team (say, three to five years out), including the capabilities and roles needed to achieve your strategy, and an overview of the development steps you plan to take to build that team. If you have already read the rest of the guide, you will have noticed that most of the steps we recommend build on processes (goal-setting sessions, periodic performance reviews, check-ins with direct reports) that are probably already part of your organization's calendar. Powered by the engagement and endorsement of the CEO and senior team, these processes will form the foundation of your leadership development effort.

We recognize that the job of developing future leaders can seem overwhelming. Where do you start? Or if you already have some activities underway, what are the most critical next steps you can take? From what we've seen others do, here are some suggestions for getting started and making progress:

- **Begin at the Beginning:** Complete our Leadership Development Diagnostic Survey, accessible online at www.bridgespan.org/LeadershipDiagnostic. It will help you determine what leadership development activities you have in place and think about how to step up to the next level.

  If you have already completed the survey, have your senior team members complete it as well and ask them to reflect on where they see the greatest challenges and opportunities for the organization. When they have done so, meet with the senior team to discuss the current status of leadership development and reach alignment on priorities for the next 12 to 18 months.

- **Engage Your Senior Leaders:** If you are a CEO just launching your leadership development efforts, begin by telling your senior team that it is important that they develop as individuals and that you'll help each of them do so. To give your words force, ask each member of the senior team to add a personal and an organizational development objective to their annual goals. In so doing, you are, in effect, incorporating leadership development into their job descriptions. Assuming you have an annual goal-setting and performance-review process, build on it—don't create something new. Use that process to hold team members accountable for progress against their leadership development objectives. Let them know that you have set development goals for yourself as well and shared them with the board, which will hold you accountable during your own annual review.

If your senior team's annual goals already include development-related items, push the process further down through the organization, beginning with the senior team's direct reports and eventually extending to the entire management team and their direct reports. Initially, to keep the process manageable, the senior team will probably want to focus on a handful of staff members. As they gain experience, they can bring all their direct reports into the process of identifying development-related goals and ensure that leadership development becomes a standard part of the goal-setting and performance evaluation process at all levels of the organization. This starts the flywheel spinning and lays the foundation for a culture of development.

Be prepared to coach and counsel those who are struggling with the work of development. You might want to role-play a goal-setting discussion and then follow up after team members meet with their direct reports. Such after-action reviews can help team members learn from the experience and apply what they've learned to future discussions. You might also bring in an outside coach to run a session for your entire senior team on this topic.

- **Understand Your Future Needs:** If this is your first foray into systematic leadership development, you can begin by gathering your senior team for a once-a-year offsite (at your house, at a board member's office—anywhere but the office) to discuss where the organization is going and the potential of their direct reports to move into more senior roles.

  Start the discussion with a perspective on where you see the organization going and what the likely leadership needs will be in three years or so—think of it as the skeleton of your Plan A. Gather feedback from your senior team and develop a common view of the key positions you'll likely need to fill and the skills and capabilities that will be required.

In discussing the potential of staff, consider using the Sample Performance-Potential Matrix tool introduced in Chapter 2. Be sure to talk about the criteria for your assessments. What constitutes "high potential," for example? If possible, calibrate your judgments by first discussing a few individuals whom your leadership team knows well. Once you've established a rough set of standards and benchmarks, you can plot more individuals and focus discussion on outliers. Who stand out clearly as future leaders? Where do you face problems? What do these individuals need in order to progress further?

Now use what you've learned from this discussion, as well as the one-on-one development conversations you are having with your senior team, to create a Plan A for your leadership team, including your thoughts on who might be potential candidates for the CEO role for the board to consider. Update the plan annually and share it with the board.

If you've already taken these steps, ask each senior team member to develop a Plan A for his or her own department. Ask them to think about how their departments' mandates are likely to evolve over time, and what competencies their teams will need to develop to succeed in the future. Consider the potential of staff members to grow into those roles—based on their own ability, engagement, and aspirations. Bear in mind that these types of forward-looking discussions can be inspiring but also emotionally charged for staff, so it's helpful to consider how to keep them positive and constructive. Include the preparation of these plans in senior team members' annual goals, and hold them accountable for doing so during annual reviews.

- **Develop Your Future Leaders:** If you're just beginning your leadership development effort, a good way to launch development is to meet twice a year with each of your direct reports to discuss his or her progress against leadership development goals. Again, don't create something new. You probably have a couple of review meetings each year to discuss progress against other goals; capitalize on these meetings by adding development goals to the agenda. In these conversations, work with each of your direct reports to identify the competencies he or she needs to develop to grow as a leader and to help the organization execute its strategy. Reach an agreement on the activities that are most likely to build those competencies, keeping the 70-20-10 framework in mind. If you've already read the rest of this guide, you'll recall that in Chapter 3 we explain how the most effective leadership learning consists of 70 percent on-the-job development supported by 20 percent coaching and mentoring, and 10 percent formal training. Working with the 70-20-10 template not only contributes to development of your senior team members but also teaches valuable Plan A lessons that they can then pass on to their direct reports.

Keep these development approaches in mind when staffing key projects or initiatives. Allocate these assignments so that staffers are doing work that develops specific leadership capabilities they need and at the same time accomplishes the organization's objectives. In doing so, you're instilling in your people the habit of thinking of projects as development opportunities.

If your leadership development program is more advanced, you can move on to building the number of talent champions in your organization, by focusing on those who are striving to become talent champions but who may need support to sharpen their talent-development skills. Model the talent development behaviors you want them to adopt by ensuring that your senior team is creating and following through on development plans with their direct reports. Consider pairing strivers with proven talent champions who can help them raise their game. It can also be helpful to develop supporting materials designed to make your managers more effective. As we describe in Chapter 3, KIPP, a leading operator of charter schools, has developed such materials to help newcomers to the management ranks understand how their perspectives and time allocations will shift as they take on more responsibility for developing their teams.

- **Hire Externally to Fill Gaps:** If your organization is new to formal leadership development, begin this process by referring back to your assessment of the organization's future leadership needs and the leadership potential of your current staff. Identify the areas where you will likely need to hire externally to meet those future needs and those where you should aim to build capacity from within. External hiring is often necessary at small- and medium-sized organizations when there is a wide management-skills gap separating, say, the finance director and the bookkeeper who reports to her. In such cases, you'll likely have to hire externally to replace the finance director—or, if the organization is growing rapidly, create a new chief financial officer role.

  If your organization's leadership development program is more advanced, you and the senior team can move from identifying potential hiring needs to considering what types of hires will constitute a good fit with your organizational culture. Chapter 4 includes a questionnaire to help you define your culture. You might want to refer to it as you consider this question. Once you have a good fix on the culture, you can think about ways of assessing a job candidate's personality and style of working and gauging whether she will fit comfortably within the culture (or in some cases give it a much-needed jolt). For starters, you might want to invite the candidate to an informal meal with you and your senior team to get better acquainted. Later, you can seek her perspective on a particular challenge facing your organization or even have her join the senior team for a work session. Such activities can give you—and the candidate—an accurate reading on the potential for a mutually beneficial partnership.

- **Monitor and Improve Your Practices:** If your leadership development program is in its initial stages, you can begin this process with three actions. First, set targets for accomplishing the work of the previous items on this list. Next, report on your organization's progress against those targets to your senior team and the board to reinforce the message of accountability. And finally, during annual goal-setting discussions with the senior team and the board, determine leadership development priorities for the coming year.

  If your organization's leadership development program is more advanced, you can work on fine-tuning your monitoring and measurement efforts. Identify particular aspects of your leadership development program to study in greater depth. Where are your efforts meeting with the least success? What kind of data can you collect to help you pinpoint the cause of the underperformance and make improvements? But don't focus exclusively on problem areas. Look for cases of "positive deviance" —aspects of the program that are meeting with better-than-expected success. Think about the information you can collect to help you understand why they're outperforming, and about how you can apply what you learn to underperforming elements of the program. And every year, expand your measuring and monitoring effort to include more elements of your leadership development program.

You may notice, once your organization has incorporated these leadership development activities into its everyday routines and rhythms, a subtle change in the culture. Leadership development finds its way into work conversations, and people begin to look at job assignments, tasks, projects, and functions not just as work to be done but also as opportunities to build leadership muscle. People start paying attention to reports on the state of the leadership pipeline in the same way they might look at reports on fundraising or membership or program participation. Skilled talent developers enjoy the respect and admiration of their peers and reports, and without really trying, the organization gains a reputation as a place where people with high potential and aspirations can make the most of their abilities. We've talked more than once in this guide about building a leadership culture, but in an important sense, the culture builds itself, as a byproduct of the organization's leadership development activities.

Another point we've made more than once is that leadership development really begins with a commitment from the CEO, whose role as chief talent officer is vital to the entire leadership development undertaking. But the CEO will need plenty of help. To take root in any organization, leadership development needs consistent, persistent engagement from its senior leadership team. Together with the CEO, they're jointly responsible for making leadership development a part of your organization's everyday business. And that means implementing the steps described in this guide in a manner that suits your organization's unique characteristics and culture. We strongly believe that the results—in the form of a stronger, more sustainable organization that's better equipped to pursue its mission—will justify the effort. As Debra Snider, vice president of operations at GuideStar, told us, "Fulfilling your mission is key, but you can't fulfill your mission unless you can sustain your organization." Or as KIPP Foundation CEO and President Richard Barth told us, "Leadership is the central premise for growing our network." We've heard similar testimonials for the value of leadership development from a wide variety of nonprofits.

We want to hear from your organization, as well. We encourage you to stay in touch with us as you take your leadership development journey by checking in at the Plan A section of the Bridgespan.org website, www.bridgespan.org/ Leadership-Development-Tools, where you'll find additional tools and resources. We also invite you to share your feedback on the guide and your suggestions for tools and practices that may be helpful to your organization and others.

# Acknowledgments

This guide would not exist without the contributions of the many nonprofits, for-profit companies, and foundations that gave generously of their time, expertise, and resources. Specifically, we'd like to thank the following nonprofits for making their CEOs and senior leaders available for interviews: Big Brothers Big Sisters of America, Boys & Girls Clubs of America, CARE USA, Communities in Schools, DonorsChoose. org, Girl Scouts of the USA, GuideStar, the KIPP Foundation, Save the Children, Teach For America, The Nature Conservancy, United Way Worldwide, Year Up, YMCA of the USA, and Youth Villages.

We also wish to acknowledge the experts from the Corporate Leadership Council, a division of the CEB, who gave freely of their time and knowledge. We would also like to thank American Express, which shared its own approach to leadership development and whose generosity allowed us to convene nonprofit CEOs, COOs, and CHROs for a discussion of their best practices and the leadership development challenges they continue to face. And we thank BoardSource for its expertise on governance.

In addition, we thank Omidyar Network, which has funded our research and provided valuable perspectives and feedback from its work with grantees on leadership development. We'd also like to thank the David and Lucile Packard Foundation for its funding, review, and input on this guide, and the Deerbrook Charitable Trust for its funding contribution.

And finally, we would like to thank our writing partner, Harris Collingwood, and our Bridgespan colleagues, with a special nod to the research team of Julia Tao, Karim Al-Khafaji, and Soumya Korde, and the knowledge team of Katie Smith Milway and Carole Matthews.

# Appendix

## Summary of steps and tools by chapter

For additional tools or to share your own, visit
www.bridgespan.org/Leadership-Development-Tools.

| Chapter | Steps | Tools |
|---------|-------|-------|
| **Engaging Your Senior Leaders** | • Step 1: Make It Clear That Leadership Development Is a Strategic Priority<br>• Step 2: Set Expectations for Senior Leaders and Hold Them Accountable<br>• Step 3: Build and Develop the Senior Team<br>• Step 4: Make the Most of Your HR Resources<br>• Step 5: Engage the Board Regularly | • Are Your Senior Leaders Engaged? An Excerpt from Our Leadership Development Diagnostic Survey<br>• Developing Others at the Y: Competency description, an excerpt from YMCA of the USA's guide to Cause-Driven Leadership®<br>• Senior Engagement at Save the Children: Conversation Calendar<br>• Questions the CEO Should Ask Each Senior Team Member about Leadership Development<br>• Questions the Board Should Ask the CEO about Leadership Development<br>• Get the Ball Rolling: Engaging Your Senior Leaders<br>• Fostering a Culture of Leadership Development |

| Chapter | Steps | Tools |
|---|---|---|
| **Understanding Your Future Needs** | • Step 1: Define the Critical Leadership Capacities Needed to Fulfill Your Organization's Mission in the Next Three to Five Years<br><br>• Step 2: Assess the Potential of Your Staff (Current and Future Leaders) to Take On Greater Responsibility<br><br>• Step 3: Create Your Plan A for What Leadership Teams within the Organization Will Look Like in Three Years | • Do You Understand Your Future Needs? An Excerpt from Our Leadership Development Diagnostic Survey<br><br>• Leadership Development Terms Defined<br><br>• Questions to Ask When Assessing Future Leadership Needs<br><br>• Sample Performance-Potential Matrix<br><br>• What "Leadership Potential" Really Means<br><br>• Sample List of Leadership Candidates and Plan A<br><br>• Building a Diverse Team to Address Future Needs<br><br>• Get the Ball Rolling: Understanding Your Future Needs |

| Chapter | Steps | Tools |
|---------|-------|-------|
| **Developing Your Future Leaders** | • Step 1: Cultivate Talent Champions<br>• Step 2: Identify Organizational Needs and Craft Development Opportunities<br>• Step 3: Co-create Individualized Development Plans<br>• Step 4: Follow Through on Development Plans | • The 70-20-10 Model<br>• Are You Effectively Developing Future Leaders? An Excerpt from Our Leadership Development Diagnostic Survey<br>• The Presence (or Lack) of Talent Champions<br>• Support for Leadership Transitions at KIPP (Excerpts from KIPP Leader Progression Road Map: Grade Level Chair to Assistant Principal)<br>• Y Sample Development Plan<br>• Get the Ball Rolling: Developing Your Future Leaders |
| **Hiring Externally to Fill Gaps** | • Step 1: Define Requirements for the Role<br>• Step 2: Create Opportunities for Both the Organization and the Candidate to Assess Whether the Candidate Is a Good Fit<br>• Step 3: Design an On-boarding Process That Supports the New Hire's Capabilities and Relationship Development | • More Help with External Hiring<br>• Are You Hiring and On-boarding Outside Leaders Effectively? An Excerpt from Our Leadership Development Diagnostic Survey<br>• Determining a Candidate's Cultural Fit<br>• Get the Ball Rolling: Hiring Externally to Fill Gaps |

| Chapter | Steps | Tools |
|---|---|---|
| **Monitoring and Improving Practices** | • Step 1: Confirm Objectives and Key Actions You're Prioritizing<br>• Step 2: Create Checkpoints to Ensure Accountability<br>• Step 3: Assess Whether You're Meeting Your Goals<br>• Step 4: Diagnose Potential Problems and Adjust Course | • Are You Monitoring Progress Effectively? An Excerpt from Our Leadership Development Diagnostic Survey<br>• Sample Leadership Development Priorities<br>• Get the Ball Rolling: Monitoring and Improving Practices<br>• Should You Compute Your Leadership Development ROI? |

# Leadership development diagnostic survey

Available online at www.bridgespan.org/LeadershipDiagnostic.

In this survey, you will be presented with 31 statements that relate to five core processes of leadership development and succession planning. For each statement, you will be asked to assess your organization's current performance in building future leaders within your organization.

| | Strongly disagree | Disagree | Agree | Strongly agree | Not applicable/ don't know |
|---|---|---|---|---|---|
| **Leadership engagement in issues around talent pipeline development** | | | | | |
| 1. Our CEO/executive director is actively engaged in building a strong pipeline of future leaders. | 1 | 2 | 3 | 4 | N/A |
| 2. Our current leaders are actively engaged in building a strong pipeline of future leaders. | 1 | 2 | 3 | 4 | N/A |
| 3. Our board members are appropriately engaged in building a strong pipeline of future leaders. | 1 | 2 | 3 | 4 | N/A |
| 4. Our current leaders are equipped to develop future leaders (e.g., trained to provide new opportunities and deliver feedback). | 1 | 2 | 3 | 4 | N/A |
| 5. Our current leaders are held accountable for building a strong pipeline of future leaders. | 1 | 2 | 3 | 4 | N/A |

| | Strongly disagree | Disagree | Agree | Strongly agree | Not applicable/ don't know |
|---|---|---|---|---|---|
| 6. Our current leaders are recognized for their efforts to develop future leaders. | 1 | 2 | 3 | 4 | N/A |
| 7. Our organizational culture supports and values leadership development. | 1 | 2 | 3 | 4 | N/A |
| 8. We invest sufficient resources (e.g., funding, time) in leadership development. | 1 | 2 | 3 | 4 | N/A |

Please provide any additional feedback or comments you have on the statements above.

**Ability to understand future talent needs**

| | Strongly disagree | Disagree | Agree | Strongly agree | Not applicable/ don't know |
|---|---|---|---|---|---|
| 9. The skills and competencies required to become a successful leader at various levels of our organization are clear. | 1 | 2 | 3 | 4 | N/A |
| 10. We have an understanding of the leadership capacity (e.g., skills and competencies, roles, and number of individuals) our organization will need 3-5 years from now in order to achieve strategic goals. | 1 | 2 | 3 | 4 | N/A |
| 11. Our employees are systematically evaluated both on their current performance and their potential to move into leadership roles. | 1 | 2 | 3 | 4 | N/A |

| | Strongly disagree | Disagree | Agree | Strongly agree | Not applicable/ don't know |
|---|---|---|---|---|---|
| 12. We have identified potential successors for critical positions. | 1 | 2 | 3 | 4 | N/A |
| 13. Where successors are not in place, we have plans in place to address our gaps. | 1 | 2 | 3 | 4 | N/A |

Please provide any additional feedback or comments you have on the statements above.

**Ability to develop future leaders**

| | Strongly disagree | Disagree | Agree | Strongly agree | Not applicable/ don't know |
|---|---|---|---|---|---|
| 14. Our performance management processes (e.g., annual evaluations, goal-setting) support effective leadership development and succession planning. | 1 | 2 | 3 | 4 | N/A |
| 15. Employees with the potential to move into leadership roles have development plans in place that identify areas for development and sources of development support. | 1 | 2 | 3 | 4 | N/A |
| 16. Employees are held accountable to and evaluated on their progress on their development plans. | 1 | 2 | 3 | 4 | N/A |
| 17. We have sufficient quality opportunities for employees to gain new leadership skills via on-the-job opportunities (e.g., stretch assignments, new projects in their existing roles). | 1 | 2 | 3 | 4 | N/A |

| | Strongly disagree | Disagree | Agree | Strongly agree | Not applicable/ don't know |
|---|---|---|---|---|---|
| 18. We have sufficient quality opportunities for employees to gain new leadership skills via mentoring and coaching. | 1 | 2 | 3 | 4 | N/A |
| 19. We have sufficient quality opportunities for employees to gain new leadership skills via formal trainings. | 1 | 2 | 3 | 4 | N/A |
| 20. The development opportunities we offer to employees (on-the-job, mentoring, training, etc.) are effective in building more capable leaders. | 1 | 2 | 3 | 4 | N/A |
| 21. Employees view our organization as a place where they can develop their leadership skills. | 1 | 2 | 3 | 4 | N/A |
| 22. When an employee moves into a leadership role, they are supported through their transition. | 1 | 2 | 3 | 4 | N/A |

Please provide any additional feedback or comments you have on the statements above.

| | Strongly disagree | Disagree | Agree | Strongly agree | Not applicable/ don't know |
|---|---|---|---|---|---|
| **Capacity around hiring and on-boarding external leaders as necessary** | | | | | |
| 23. We hire from external sources primarily when the capabilities required for a position are difficult to develop internally. | 1 | 2 | 3 | 4 | N/A |
| 24. External candidates seeking leadership roles are attracted to our organization. | 1 | 2 | 3 | 4 | N/A |
| 25. We effectively screen external leadership candidates to ensure they are correct for the role and organization. | 1 | 2 | 3 | 4 | N/A |
| 26. We on-board and successfully integrate external leadership hires. | 1 | 2 | 3 | 4 | N/A |
| Please provide any additional feedback or comments you have on the statements above. | | | | | |
| **Ability to measure and improve leadership development practices** | | | | | |
| 27. We have established clear goals to guide our leadership development efforts. | 1 | 2 | 3 | 4 | N/A |
| 28. We regularly collect data about our leadership development practices to understand whether they are effective. | 1 | 2 | 3 | 4 | N/A |

| | Strongly disagree | Disagree | Agree | Strongly agree | Not applicable/ don't know |
|---|---|---|---|---|---|
| 29. We take action on the data we collect to improve our leadership development practices. | 1 | 2 | 3 | 4 | N/A |
| 30. As changes to organizational strategy occur, we update our leadership development goals and practices accordingly. | 1 | 2 | 3 | 4 | N/A |
| Please provide any additional feedback or comments you have on the statements above. | | | | | |
| **Summary** | | | | | |
| 31. All things considered, our organization is highly effective in developing a strong internal and external pipeline of future leaders. | 1 | 2 | 3 | 4 | N/A |

# Leadership Development Diagnostic – The Role of the Board

This survey tool is intended for use by board members of nonprofit organizations and their CEOs. It reflects input from over 150 board members and CEOs on the role of the board in supporting leadership development; it will help you assess the effectiveness of the board across four critical areas of support. For this survey and other tools, please go to www.bridgespan.org/Leadership-Development-Tools.

| | Strongly disagree | Disagree | Agree | Strongly agree | Not applicable/ don't know |
|---|---|---|---|---|---|
| **CEO evaluation, development & succession** | | | | | |
| 1. The board leads the CEO hiring process. | 1 | 2 | 3 | 4 | N/A |
| 2. The board conducts an annual evaluation of the CEO. | 1 | 2 | 3 | 4 | N/A |
| 3. The board's evaluation of the CEO considers how well s/he is developing current and future leaders of the organization. | 1 | 2 | 3 | 4 | N/A |
| 4. The board helps the CEO identify his/her own professional development goals. | 1 | 2 | 3 | 4 | N/A |
| 5. The board reviews the CEO's compensation annually. | 1 | 2 | 3 | 4 | N/A |
| 6. The board collaborates with the CEO to develop his/her succession plan. | 1 | 2 | 3 | 4 | N/A |

| | Strongly disagree | Disagree | Agree | Strongly agree | Not applicable/ don't know |
|---|---|---|---|---|---|
| 7. The board reviews the CEO's succession plan annually. | 1 | 2 | 3 | 4 | N/A |

Please provide any additional feedback or comments you have on the statements above.

## Senior leadership team development & succession

| | Strongly disagree | Disagree | Agree | Strongly agree | Not applicable/ don't know |
|---|---|---|---|---|---|
| 8. In some cases, the board provides input on candidates for senior leadership positions. | 1 | 2 | 3 | 4 | N/A |
| 9. The board ensures there are succession plans in place for other senior leadership positions. | 1 | 2 | 3 | 4 | N/A |
| 10. The board encourages leaders (in addition to the CEO) to actively participate in board meetings. | 1 | 2 | 3 | 4 | N/A |

Please provide any additional feedback or comments you have on the statements above.

## Leadership development processes & resources

| | Strongly disagree | Disagree | Agree | Strongly agree | Not applicable/ don't know |
|---|---|---|---|---|---|
| 11. When developing the organization's strategy the board provides input on what leadership roles and capabilities may be needed in the future. | 1 | 2 | 3 | 4 | N/A |

| | Strongly disagree | Disagree | Agree | Strongly agree | Not applicable/ don't know |
|---|---|---|---|---|---|
| 12. When budgeting, the board allocates funds to support the development of the CEO and other current or future leaders. | 1 | 2 | 3 | 4 | N/A |
| 13. The board ensures the organization has processes in place for developing current and future leaders. | 1 | 2 | 3 | 4 | N/A |
| Please provide any additional feedback or comments you have on the statements above. | | | | | |

### Goal-setting & monitoring

| | | | | | |
|---|---|---|---|---|---|
| 14. The board ensures the organization has leadership development goals in place. | 1 | 2 | 3 | 4 | N/A |
| 15. The board reviews the organization's performance against its leadership development goals annually. | 1 | 2 | 3 | 4 | N/A |
| Please provide any additional feedback or comments you have on the statements above. | | | | | |

### Summary

| | | | | | |
|---|---|---|---|---|---|
| 16. All things considered, the board is appropriately engaged in the development of current and future leaders for our organization. | 1 | 2 | 3 | 4 | N/A |

# Additional resources

- Adams, Thomas H. *The Nonprofit Leadership Transition and Development Guide: Proven Paths for Leaders and Organizations.* San Francisco: Jossey-Bass, 2010. Print.

- American Express NGen Fellows. "Changing the Status Quo: Intentional Succession Planning Through Leadership Development." *IndependentSector.org.* Independent Sector, June 2011. Web. (www.independentsector.org/2010_ngen_fellows_project).

- Barner, Robert. *Bench Strength: Developing the Depth and Versatility of Your Organization's Leadership Talent.* New York: AMACOM/American Management Association, 2006. Print.

- The Bridgepsan Group. "Finding Leaders for America's Nonprofits: Commentaries." *Bridgespan.org.* The Bridgespan Group, 20 Apr. 2009. Web. (www.bridgespan.org).

- The Bridgespan Group. "52 Free Development Opportunities for Nonprofit Staff." *Bridgespan.org.* The Bridgespan Group, 2011. Web. (www.bridgespan.org).

- The Bridgespan Group. "On-boarding: Tips for Transitioning into a Senior Nonprofit Role." *Bridgespan.org.* The Bridgespan Group, 2010. Web. (www.bridgespan.org).

- Cappelli, Peter. "Talent Management for the Twenty-First Century." *Harvard Business Review* (2008). 1 Mar. 2008. Web.

- Cermak, Jenny, and Monica McGurk. "Putting a Value on Training." *McKinsey Quarterly* (2010). July 2010. Web.

- Charan, Ram. "Ending the CEO Succession Crisis." *Harvard Business Review* (2005). Feb. 2005. Web.

- Charan, Ram, Stephen J. Drotter, and James L. Noel. *The Leadership Pipeline: How to Build the Leadership-powered Company.* San Francisco: Jossey-Bass, 2001. Print.

- Cohn, Jeffrey M., Rakesh Khurana, and Laura Reeves. "Growing Talent as If Your Business Depended on It." *Harvard Business Review* (2005). Print.

- Conger, Jay A., and Robert M. Fulner. "Developing Your Leadership Pipeline." *Harvard Business Review* (2009). Print.

- Cornelius, Maria, Patrick Corvington, and Albert Ruesga. "Ready to Lead?: Next Generation Leaders Speak Out." *Meyerfoundation.org.* The Annie E. Casey Foundation, Meyer Foundation, Idealist.org, and CompassPoint Nonprofit Services, 2008. Web. (www.meyerfoundation.org).

- Cornelius, Maria, Rick Moyers, and Jeanne Bell. "Daring to Lead." *Daringtolead.org.* CompassPoint Nonprofit Services & Meyer Foundation, 2011. Web. (www.daringtolead.org).

# Appendix

- CEB. *How Growing Organizations Develop Leaders.* Publication. CEB, Feb. 2009. Web. (newprofit.com/binary-data/LINK/file/000/000/379-1.pdf).
- Drucker, Adam, Beth Gonzales, Selena Juneau-Vogel, Monisha Makhijani, and Michael Turi. "Developing Senior Management Diversity." National Human Services Assembly, Spring 2011. Web.
- Forman, David C. "Establishing a Talent-Driven Culture." Sundt.com. Human Capital Institute, 2009. Web.
- Gay, Matthew, and Doris M. Sims. *Building Tomorrow's Talent: A Practitioner's Guide to Talent Management and Succession Planning.* Bloomington, IN: AuthorHouse, 2006. Print.
- Groysberg, Boris, Scott A. Snook, and David Lane. "Pine Street Initiative at Goldman Sachs." *Harvard Business School* (2006). Harvard Business Review, 14 Nov. 2006. Web. (www.hbr.org).
- Lombardo, Michael M. and Robert W. Eichinger. *FYI For Your Improvement: A Guide for Development and Coaching (for Learners, Managers, Mentors, and Feedback Givers).* Lominger International: A Koren/Ferry Company, 1996-2009. Print.
- Nelson, Stephen J. "Do You Know What's in Your Leadership Pipeline?" *Harvard Business Review* (2002). 1 May 2002. Web.
- Rothwell, William J. *Effective Succession Planning: Ensuring Leadership Continuity and Building Talent from Within.* New York: AMACOM, 2010. Print.
- Schwartz, Robert, James Weinberg, Dana Hagenbuch, and Allison Scott. "The Voice of Nonprofit Talent: Perceptions of Diversity in the Workplace." Commongood Careers & Level Playing Field Institute. Web. (www.cgcareers.org/articles/detail/the-voice-of-nonprofit-talent-diversity-in-the-workplace/).
- Tierney, Thomas J. "The Nonprofit Sector's Leadership Deficit White Paper." *Bridgespan.org.* The Bridgespan Group, 19 June 2006. Web. (www.bridgespan.org).
- Wolfred, Tom. "Building Leaderful Organizations: Succession Planning for Nonprofits." AECF.org. The Annie E. Casey Foundation, 2008. Web. (www.aecf.org).
- Wolfred, Tom. "Succession Planning for Nonprofits of All Sizes." *BlueAvocado.org.* 2009. Web. (www.blueavocado.org).

Made in the USA
Charleston, SC
27 November 2013